Intuitive Adventures

Beyond the Camera Lens

Aloha

*Digital photo design by
L.Clifford Norager*

*"The most beautiful experience we
can have is the mysterious"*

Albert Einstein

INTUITIVE ADVENTURES
BEYOND THE CAMERA LENS

Written by Diane E. Zander
Photographs taken by Diane E. Zander
Edited by Karen Valentine, Eric Langberg, & Merav Reid
Copy Editing/Proof Reading by Alessandra Ruper-Weber
Graphics Consultant by L.Clifford Norager

Intuitive Guidance, Where From?

Intuitive guidance, where from?
Dare you open yourself to a life that is trusting?
Trusting the unknown, but challenging the boundaries!

Excitement of discoveries shared…
Admiring the beauty of created creatures,
In touch with nature, reflecting on meaning…

Aware of multidimensional experiences
Not judging spiritual realms
Thinking outside the box…

Adventures that allow for miracles
Flowing with time and place
Listening, hearing, seeing beyond…

Receiving healing, listening to the inner voice
Experiencing new connectedness within,
Deep inner peace and contentment…

Trusting Divine revealing guidance
Illuminating inner soul's visionary dreams
These are intuitive adventures, gifts of life!

Poem by Merav Reid (© 2010)

Copyright © 2010, 2011 Diane E. Zander.

All rights reserved. No part of this book may be used or reproduced by any means, graphic, electronic, or mechanical, including photocopying, recording, taping or by any information storage retrieval system without the written permission of the publisher except in the case of brief quotations embodied in critical articles and reviews.

Balboa Press books may be ordered through booksellers or by contacting:

Balboa Press
A Division of Hay House
1663 Liberty Drive
Bloomington, IN 47403
www.balboapress.com
1-(877) 407-4847

Because of the dynamic nature of the Internet, any web addresses or links contained in this book may have changed since publication and may no longer be valid. The views expressed in this work are solely those of the author and do not necessarily reflect the views of the publisher, and the publisher hereby disclaims any responsibility for them.

ISBN: 978-1-4525-3410-7 (sc)
ISBN: 978-1-4525-4068-9 (e)

Library of Congress Control Number: 2011910735

Any people depicted in stock imagery provided by Thinkstock are models, and such images are being used for illustrative purposes only. Certain stock imagery © Thinkstock.

Printed in the United States of America

Balboa Press rev. date: 11/1/2011

BOOK REVIEWS

In her book *Intuitive Adventures – beyond the Camera Lens*, Diane E. Zander takes the reader along a journey of self-discovery. The book encompasses a mosaic of experiences, which Diane shares with enthusiasm and excitement. One of the highlights is her work on Photographic Energy Phenomena (PEP): unusual white or transparent balls appearing in photos, which represent a bridge between the spiritual realms and photographic imagery. Diane's book is captivating. I would recommend it to everyone who, like her, embraces the unknown and makes it a passion.

>Dr. Cairo Rocha; author of *Emotions and the Hidden Link*

A sincere account of one soul's dedicated journey to find the guiding light in life.

>Alan Cohen; author of *A Deep Breath of Life*

Diane's quest to follow her intuition, literally at all costs, is a fabulous example for the rest of us. If we trust our inner guidance, the Path is always revealed and we never have to worry. This book is in the "can't put it down" category—a combination of fascinating stories, terrific writing and wonderful photos, with the final reward being a confirmation of inner Knowing that all our needs are taken care of; all we need is to surrender and open our hearts.

>Barbara Garcia; Co-Publisher <u>*Ke Ola Magazine*</u>
>
>*Celebrating the Arts, Culture & Sustainability of Hawaii Island*

Contents

Acknowledgements viii

Introduction: Opening the Door to Self-Expression ix

Chapter 1: A New Way 1

Chapter 2: Forgiveness Begins within my Heart 6

Chapter 3: A Miraculous Healing 10

Chapter 4: Ayahuasca: The Sacred Medicine Plant 13

Chapter 5: The Calling 16

Chapter 6: A Mystical Encounter in Montezuma 18

Chapter 7: Farewell New Jersey 21

Chapter 8: Moving to Hawaii: Crossing the Threshold 23

Chapter 9: The Photographic Energy Phenomena 26

Chapter 10: The Dolphins' Loving Presence 31

Chapter 11: The Horse with No Name 33

Chapter 12: Return to India 35

Chapter 13: Emigrating to New Zealand 38

Chapter 14: Message in the Cloud 40

Chapter 15: The Mystifying Face in Peru 45

Chapter 16: The Spirit of the Fire 49

Chapter 17: The Cross of Light Phenomena 53

Epilogue: The Heart of the Moon, Again! 58

About The Author 59

Acknowledgements

First and foremost I would like to thank my family and especially my mother, who I now believe sits on my shoulder and lovingly watches over me each and every day. Thanks, Mom, for rescuing me and providing unconditional love when I hated life and became a troubled rebel in my teens and early adult life. And by the way, Mom…thank you so much for sending me the sign of the full moon transformed into a heart. I am so glad all is well in Heaven for you!

My deepest gratitude to Eric Langberg, Karen Valentine, Merav Reid, and Alessandra Ruper-Weber for their relentless dedication in editing *Intuitive Adventures beyond the Camera Lens*. Without your help and guidance, this book would not be possible.

Many thanks for all the teachers and healers who crossed my path and were instrumental in my healing. I have the deepest reverence for those who devote their lives to helping others.

My sincere appreciation for all the animals and plants that have profoundly touched my heart: especially Delia, Sunshine and Ayahuasca.

Heartfelt thanks to Ofelia Dulko and Chantal Guillou Brennan for your love and support.

With gratitude for all the many wonderful people I have met and shared sacred space with during my grand adventures traveling around the world.

Thanks to all the amazing friends in my life; human, as well as celestial, for sharing your Love and Light with me.

With profound and continuing gratitude to God, Creator of All That Is, for communing with my intuition and leading me to slowly fulfill my life purpose on Planet Earth.

Introduction

"I wish to portray how life can be incredibly exciting and a wonderful discovery of trusting one's intuition and God's guidance through every difficulty and blessing."

Heart Moon

Opening the Door to Self-Expression

Aloha! My name is Diane, also known as *Heart Moon*. This book, *Intuitive Adventures beyond the Camera Lens,* is a true story chronicling my surprising and enlightening journey into the unknown realms of self-healing and self-discovery. I achieved this experience at high cost by daring to delve deep within the depths of my soul—a journey that has included facing death on numerous occasions.

With divine inspiration guiding a series of remarkable adventures, I experienced and photographed rare and unique light phenomena that I decided to call Photographic Energy Phenomena or PEP. I believe that light contains both information and transformative energy, which can be captured and displayed with photography. The result is a series of mystifying images demonstrating this energy. The acronym PEP is used throughout this book to describe one or more examples of these light forms. Delving into their meaning and purpose, in recent years I've integrated these celestial apparitions into a practice of healing and reflected wisdom. Gazing at PEP has provided countless, helpful and life-changing insights for many people, including myself.

For the past 13 years, I have been on a remarkable mission of self–discovery, pursuing my own life's *soul* purpose after leaving a successful nursing career and giving up worldly possessions to move to Hawai'i and to New Zealand. Igniting this journey was a confrontation with an excruciatingly painful issue that forced me to explore my inner world. I vowed to search deep into my heart and resolve all self-limiting and paralyzing, childhood beliefs that I found kept me from having total peace of mind. I literally implored, "God, the Creator of all that is, heal me, so I may be of greater service to humanity." Setting this daily intention has not only created some tormenting and harrowing moments, but it has also meant connecting to a multitude of awe-inspiring people, places and events beyond my wildest dreams!

Oh what extraordinary, divinely-guided journeys I have led.

Among them are a mystifying experience with Jesus and Kuan Yin in Costa Rica; a profound connection with the Aboriginal people in Australia; a challenge to remain calm while being surrounded and spied upon by Chinese military in Tibet; divine encounters with dolphins and humpback whales; explorations of the Egyptian Sphinx and the Great Pyramids; connecting with indigenous shamans in Peru, who helped me heal my heart chakra, and finally becoming an instrument for sharing divine Love through my Photographic Energy Phenomena or PEP.

In writing *Intuitive Adventures beyond the Camera Lens*, I have been asked how I felt when I received a miraculous healing in the High Andes or when I was confronted by death during a vision quest in the Amazon rainforest. How was I changed after visiting a Zulu shaman in South Africa during the September 11, 2001, Twin Towers attack, when so many lives were lost, yet I received a profound message of peace? What life lessons did I learn when I escaped death again in India and gained profound wisdom about the power of shining my Light instead of allowing self-pity?

After reading *Intuitive Adventures beyond the Camera Lens*, I would pose to the reader, for consideration, two questions about living in this age of great uncertainty:

• Are you prepared to cope with how this world's trauma may affect you physically, psychologically and spiritually?

• Are you apt to "fall apart," or are you going to trust your intuition to guide you through at all cost?

It continues to be an incredible honor helping others—through my photographs—to discover their own peace of mind and contentment, as I have had the courage to delve deep into my own heart and bring forth my truth, no matter what other people think. This would not have been possible without the help of that divine inner voice and the Photographic Energy Phenomena.

As you gaze at the photographs in this book, the images may convey powerful messages to you. I invite you to open your heart to this fascinating new field of understanding.

Enjoy,

Heart Moon

Diane E. Zander—*Heart Moon*—is a Registered Nurse, specializing in behavioral health, Reiki Master, Inspirational Teacher and Intuitive Photographer.

Chapter 1

*"Someday perhaps the inner Light will shine forth from us,
and we'll need no other Light."*
Johann Wolfgang von Goethe

A New Way

The PEP seemed to have relocated somewhere else or disappeared. How mystifying!

Niue (pronounced "New Way") is a small, remote tropical island three and a half hours by air northeast of Nelson, New Zealand where I lived for awhile during 2007. It is one of only three places in the world I know of where you can legally swim with the humpback whales.

I booked a three-month accommodation in the small village of Avatele, just south of Alofi, the capital of Niue.

Soon after arriving early in June, I was told by local fishermen that it would most likely be about three or four weeks before we sighted the first humpback whales. The Southern Humpback Whales leave their feeding grounds in Antarctica and migrate north to the tropical waters of the South Pacific to mate and give birth from late June to October. In the meantime, I was happy to have some time to settle in and connect with the land and the local people.

Island life on Niue is extremely low-key. The locals take life as it comes—nice and slow and easy. The lush, virgin forests and black-coral reefs that jut out from the shoreline are eye-catchers. The ocean is so crystal-clear you can easily see 70 feet below the surface. Niue is a true haven for snorkelers who have a passion to swim with humpback whales and anyone longing for a peaceful, enchanting getaway.

Winter is usually the dry, calm season when the weather is generally perfect. During my stay, however, we experienced a few unpredictable thunderstorms, producing rough, pounding seas, frightening lightning strikes and electrical blackouts. The storms knocked out phone service for weeks and slowed the Internet connection to a snail's pace. These situations reminded me that I was not on some "time clock" with matters needing my immediate attention, such as when I was working as a nurse. I also had to remind myself to consciously breathe! I was quite taken aback as to how conditioned I had become to expecting immediate gratification and instant answers to my problems.

A few days after arriving on Niue, I took a short walk down the narrow dirt road to the boat ramp at Avatele Beach. There, in the middle of the boat ramp parking lot, I noticed a beautiful, multi-colored kitten sitting peacefully. Seeing me, she immediately got up and started walking in my direction. I looked around the area for a mother cat, but there was none to be seen. After giving the kitten a hug and saying goodbye, I started walking back to the cottage. To my surprise, when I turned around I realized she had followed me home.

My newfound friend immediately started meowing about my feet, apparently hungry. With no cat food in the house, she gratefully ate some brown rice and beans. She had already made herself at home. Since every time I looked at her I smiled, I decided to call her "Sunshine."

The next day, I borrowed a bike from the property manager and rode the ten kilometers into town to buy cat food. The ride was grueling for two reasons: the bike was quite old, with gears rusted from the saltwater, causing them to not work very well or not at all; and, secondly, I was a little out of shape. Well, maybe a lot out of shape!

After finally arriving in town, I saw a sign on the grocery store door saying, "Sorry We Are Closed." In frustration, I turned around to go back, and on the way I noticed a small roadside stand that was open. "No we don't have cat food," said the Niuean owner with a friendly smile, "but we do sell canned tuna fish."

"Great," I say. That night Sunshine gobbled the tuna fish right down and then jumped on my lap, purring peacefully.

A couple of weeks later, while outside reading in the hammock, I noticed the neighbor's cat checking out Sunshine. Right in front of my eyes, the cat dashed like a "runaway train" toward Sunshine, mounted her, and immediately ran back to his house.

Well, about a month later, noticing Sunshine's plump little belly, I realized that my innocent young pet was pregnant. I was outraged! How dare that cat do this to Sunshine! It sent me reeling back in time to the moment I lost my innocence as a teenager. During a drinking episode, an older male, a so-called friend, took sexual advantage of my vulnerability. This painful experience with Sunshine created in me an opportunity to heal an inner wound.

Every evening, Sunshine and I would sit outside in my hammock and gaze at the twinkling stars, wondering about the universe and its mysteries. It was there that my connection with the Photographic Energy Phenomena or PEP began.

On most nights I would feel the urge to take hundreds of photos. My belief is that the photographs containing the PEP are capturing energies from the spiritual world that would like to be able to connect with us. Before clicking away with my camera, I humbly ask the PEP to please reveal themselves to me. Sometimes I have an *intuitive knowing* of their presence. What is important to me is that I never feel apprehensive or threatened by them. I believe they come in love, and I feel blessed to be able to connect with their world.

A typical evening at my Niue cottage; Sunshine, the PEP and Diane

One night Sunshine was walking around the yard, acting as if there were something attracting her attention. I decided to take a photo of her and was quite amazed at what I saw in the viewfinder: a PEP above Sunshine's head. "Wow, Sunshine, I don't think we are alone!"

Sunshine with a PEP above her head.

The neighbor's dog frequently stopped by to visit Sunshine and me. I didn't know his name, so I decided to call him Rover. During one of his visits on our porch, he suddenly stood up and ran toward the palm tree in the front yard. I picked up my camera and started clicking away. To my pleasant surprise, I saw a PEP on Rover's left hind leg, and, in the very next photo, it seemed to have relocated somewhere else or disappeared. How very interesting!

PEP on Rover's left hind leg.

PEP either disappeared or relocated elsewhere.

Here are examples of the PEP behavior. When I immediately snapped another photo, these particular PEP either disappeared or relocated to another area.

Here a large PEP is seen on the branch of a tree.

The large PEP has now disappeared.

You can also see other less defined PEP in these photos.

Again the PEP appears to be moving around. Only a few seconds elapsed between these two photos.

These phenomena fascinated me so much that I decided to continue exploring and documenting these unusual appearances of PEP as well as their behavior. (See subsequent chapters for more information about the PEP and how to connect with them.)

In the Eye of the Humpback

By mid-July, only a few whales had been seen, way off-shore, and I was becoming increasingly disappointed. Every day, I would walk to the black coral beach and gaze out towards the open sea, looking for humpback whales.

With frustration building inside me, I had to keep reminding myself to be patient and trust that they would come. Every day I contacted the Niue Dive Shop only to get disappointing updates.

My friend Steve was soon coming to visit from California and I pleaded with God many times over, "Please God, let us have some amazing encounters with the whales. Steve is spending a lot of money to come and swim with these magnificent beings of the sea. So please God, and I repeat…*Please*, at least do it for him!"

Optimistically we decided to book reservations to go out on the boat for four days, starting with the Saturday after his arrival, hoping that we would see and swim with the humpback whales.

I picked up Steve at the airport at the ungodly hour of 3 a.m. on a Friday. After a short sleep, breakfast and catching up with each other, we walked to the beach a few minutes away, where we planned to launch the old, heavy kayak lying there. Tugging and dragging the old rickety kayak towards the water, I just happened to look out towards the sea. "Wow, there she blows!" I exclaimed, sounding like a local who has just experienced a humpback sighting very close by.

We literally dropped the kayak and dove into the water, swimming out past the channel to the open and expansive sea. We sang, laughed and swam for about an hour before sighting another whale. Then, unexpectedly, out of nowhere—and I mean *out of nowhere*—two huge humpbacks breached out of the water right next to us. "Oh my God! What a WOW!" They swam around us for a minute or two and then…off they went! Steve and I looked at each other in utter amazement. What a greeting! After this serendipitous experience, we just knew we were going to have a fantastic week.

Every day we went out in the boat, the whales welcomed us as we swam with them, sharing their love and peaceful presence with us. One day, two female humpbacks swam within a few feet, and lingered intimately with both of us for at least 30 minutes. One of them gazed directly into my eye, into my soul, for about 20 seconds. It is very difficult to describe in words how I felt swimming with these magnificent beings, but if I am to describe the experience, the word "bliss" comes to mind. "I thank you, humpback whales, for your beautiful expression of divine Love."

The eye of love

As the week flew by we had an incredibly fun time swimming with the whales and sharing our stories. Steve and I both felt sad that Mary, his wife, couldn't come. Every time we were with the whales, we sent her love and light. I am truly ecstatic and grateful knowing that God responds to heartfelt prayers.

After Steve left, the humpbacks appeared offshore only occasionally. I so yearned for their love, looking for them daily, I asked with tears running down my cheeks, "Where are you? Where have you gone? I miss you so!"

Weeks later while meditating, I understood what the whales were trying to teach me. "Seek the love you are looking for within. Looking for the love outside yourself is just temporary." I didn't necessarily want to hear this, but I knew it was my truth.

As I was preparing to leave Niue, while talking to one of the boat owners at their shop, suddenly I heard a flapping noise as two humpback whales swam close to the shore and gave us a remarkable, acrobatic display. I believe it was their way of saying goodbye to me. Again, tears running down my face, I sent them my heartfelt love in return, wishing them a safe journey back to the waters of Antarctica.

The day I left, I was overwhelmed with sadness because Sunshine had not yet given birth, and it was very difficult to leave her after spending months together. She would lay quietly on my chest in the hammock each morning while I meditated. Joanna, my neighbor, promised me that she and her family would take good care of Sunshine. A couple of weeks later, I learned that Sunshine had safely delivered several kittens the day after I left. Bursting with joy I said, "Thank goodness!" as the tears rolled down my face. I sure do love my little Sunshine, even though it is now from a distance.

To detach with love has been one of the most difficult lessons in my life. I am finding how important it is to cherish and embrace the love I am receiving in the moment it happens. The emotional highs and lows of living in Niue taught me many powerful insights about life and the way I process my feelings. The humpback whales taught me to look within to seek the love I am yearning for.

Chapter 2

> "Lord make me an instrument of thy peace.
> Where there is hatred, let me sow love."
> St. Francis of Assisi

Forgiveness Begins within my Heart

"You son of a bitch!" he yelled to me as he got in his truck and proceeded to race down the dirt road like a crazy man.

In 1997, when my nursing career was in full swing, I was confronted with a core issue erupting inside of me. It began forcing itself to the surface, like an internal explosion. As with many women (and men), this is a story that begins with my mother, whom I still love very deeply.

My mom

When Mom was in her late 70s and beginning to have difficulty with the upkeep of her property, I decided to return home to help. I was in my mid-40s, single and feeling deeply connected to the land. Mom had supported me through my turbulent times and I thought this would be a way to give back to her.

As I adjusted to my new living situation, I developed a deep love for gardening and began planting flowering bushes and creating unique rock gardens in the backyard. I found it nurtured my soul while connecting me with Mother Nature's beauty.

All went well for about a year, until the undeveloped property next to ours was sold, and I soon became very concerned. I knew that the new owners had a "right of way" to pass through our property to get to theirs. Living on a private road, there were no municipal traffic laws that could be enforced and it would be difficult to prevent the neighbor from doing whatever he wanted on that road, without taking legal action.

Initially, the new homeowner (we will call him Max) and I became friendly acquaintances. Unfortunately this was short-lived. We both had strong egos. He was tall, stocky, and intimidating. When he didn't get his way, his anger would pour out of him like a raging bull. Max triggered my own unresolved anger issues, which began surfacing after our first disagreement.

One autumn day, Max and I were talking about the property and right-of-way laws. The discussion became heated, egos clashed, and angry outbursts followed. "You son of a bitch!" he yelled to me as he got into his truck and proceeded to race down the dirt road like a crazy man.

As years passed, our relationship continued to deteriorate and Max became even more verbally abusive and threatening towards me. There were many rumors around the neighborhood about his vindictive nature, and I would cringe when I heard the stories, which heightened my anxiety towards him.

Friends would say, "Pray for him." I couldn't. Love thy neighbor? No way! The heck with that! How could I possibly pray for someone whom I thought was abusive, hateful, vengeful and arrogant?

Becoming increasingly afraid of him, my animosity towards Max began keeping me from feeling secure in my own home. My heart would pound as he raced his car past me, and I feared for my dogs, who also felt the tension and wanted to chase after him. It wasn't easy restraining a large Rottweiler on a leash. Horrifying thoughts would race through my mind. I believed that, if given the opportunity, he would run over them and not think twice about it. Unfortunately the police couldn't enforce the 20-mile-per-hour residential speed limit because it was a private road.

My ego would not allow me to ignore Max and his tyrannical behavior. The stress and anxiety began to affect my health. I developed vertigo, which often rendered me powerless with symptoms such as extreme dizziness and nausea, causing me to stop in my tracks and lie down until they subsided. I look back now and wonder if my guardian angel was trying to teach me a lesson. Was my health problem related to emotional issues of control? Was I getting sick, behaving like Max and feeling I needed to be in control at all times?

I finally decided to just ignore Max, as difficult as it was when the sight of him speeding down the road in his high-powered, four-wheel drive truck sent chills throughout my body. I so wanted to react! A new shift needed to happen between us. It was time to not be afraid of him. I knew he wasn't going to change; I needed to change my attitude towards him. I finally took the advice of a friend who had been telling me for years to pray for him. So, every time he would race past my driveway, I began sending him loving energy.

About a year later, I truly began to feel compassion towards Max as a result of the loving thoughts I had been sending him. My priorities were shifting and I began feeling drawn toward more spiritual ways of thinking. Mysticism intrigued me. I started to address issues of fear, control, and anger and began realizing how these negative emotions were interfering with my happiness.

It was during this time in my life that Mom's health was starting to decline. Even though she was still spunky, outgoing and independent at the young age of 85 years, this all changed one cold autumn day in 1997. While taking her usual daily walk, she tripped and fell head first, hitting her face on the pavement. Mom lay in the street, unconscious, until a neighbor found her and called for help. At the time, I had no idea how this accident would end up changing my life dramatically.

I was unaware of what had happened until later that night when my brother called me at work. Fortunately, Mom had been taken to the hospital where I worked. I was shocked when I first saw her lying there in the hospital bed. This formerly proud, powerful, strong-willed woman now looked like a helpless, innocent child. The bruises, cuts, swollen eyes, and head trauma immediately brought tears to my eyes and fear consumed me. I said in a stern tone to myself, "Toughen up. You are a nurse; you can fix her!" Wanting to make all the pain and suffering go away, I did my best to comfort and reassure her.

Mom would say to me, "Diane, I want to go home now; you can take care of me at home." One of her worst fears was being hospitalized, but she needed to stay there a couple of weeks until the doctor felt she was stable enough to leave. I stayed with her almost constantly, whenever I was not working, until she was discharged.

Over the following months, Mom's health rapidly declined, and she became increasingly dependent, soon requiring almost constant care. For many months I was her primary caregiver and struggled, wishing I could fix her. I prayed and bargained with God for her recovery, but to no avail. It was heart-wrenching when God kept saying to me, "No."

I didn't want my mom to die. She couldn't die. What would I do without her? She meant the world to me. Watching her slowly deteriorate and become helpless was unbearable; my heart literally ached. My anxiety began to intensify; fear and control issues were again surfacing. Stress began to outwardly express itself, turning my neck into one big, tight knot. I was having difficulty concentrating at work, where I was attempting to control everyone and everything. Feeling powerless and extremely insecure, I began to realize that I was the one out of control.

My partner at that time was getting quite concerned and suggested we go to a health spa for the weekend. Tired of feeling the effects of stress and anxiety, I agreed, knowing Mom would be in good hands with the live-in home aide we had recently hired. Initially it was very difficult persuading her to have a live-in. "Diane, you know I don't like having strangers in our home. You can do it." I had to remind her, over and over again, that I was working full time and wasn't "Wonder Woman."

Off we went on our weekend getaway, despite some resistance from my mom. At this point, she was emotionally dependent on me. Her anxiety and fear of dying had continued to intensify.

Over the weekend, I received many spa treatments, but the neck pain would not go away. The day we were to return home, I was offered a Reiki treatment. At the time I was somewhat skeptical of this practice but, feeling desperate, I accepted.

To my surprise, I was profoundly affected. My neck pain decreased considerably and what really impressed me was how I felt emotionally. I was experiencing a peace that I had never known before. All my life I wanted to have a *knowing*, a heartfelt knowing that there was something greater than myself—a Presence some call God, Holy Spirit, Higher Self, Oneness—guiding me for my highest good. Reiki opened that door. I knew at that point I wanted to learn more about Reiki and the healing effects it offered.

I attended a workshop at the local hospital and received my First Level training in Reiki. A few days later, I began using Reiki daily on myself. I knew it would not be a quick fix to release the blocked energy, because I had so many issues to deal with. Reiki helped me to foster peaceful, loving thoughts and feelings. As the months passed, I was confronting my fears and also offered Reiki to my mom.

She seemed calmer after receiving Reiki healings from me and was able to talk about dying without having an anxiety attack. One of the hardest things I ever did was to give Mom permission to die. Her response was, "I can't die yet. I still need to take care of you!" This must have been hard for her as she had always been in the role of a mother protecting her children. I felt it was Mom's denial surfacing and her way of avoiding her knowledge of impending death.

My relationship with her grew and deepened as the days passed. During one of our many conversations about life after death, I asked Mom to give me a sign after she had passed—and not just an ordinary sign—to tell me that all was well in Heaven for her.

She went into a coma on March 1, 1999, and for the next few days I stayed by her side, watching and painfully listening to her labored breathing. One day I yelled out to God, "Please take her now! I can't handle seeing her this way!" With tears running down my face, to my surprise, a few moments later Mom took her last breath and made her transition from this Earth. I cried for days afterwards.

Even though the aftermath of her falling was the most difficult time in my life, it became a time of profound healing. I had to learn the extremely difficult lesson of surrendering completely to God without in some way trying to control the outcome. Gratefully, I can truly say I am not the same person I was before her accident.

Some time after Mom's passing, I learned that Max had undergone triple bypass heart surgery. I guess all those years of being angry and full of rage had caught up with him. For some strange reason, I felt sorry for him. I realized that the Reiki love I was sending to him over the past year was also helping me to get in touch with my compassionate side. I decided to send Max a get-well card, even though it was ironic that the thought of sending this tyrant a get-well card even two years earlier would never, ever have entered my mind.

Two weeks later, while taking my dogs for a walk, Max drove up to me, stopped his car and said in a gruff tone, "Diane that was a beautiful card you sent me." At that moment I had tears in my eyes. He said, "Let's forget the past. It's over with." We talked about his heart surgery and how frightening it was for him. We hugged—yes *hugged*—before we said goodbye. Over the next couple of months we developed a friendly relationship. He even accepted my offer, as a nurse, to teach him how to take his own blood pressure and monitor medications.

During this time, I gained much insight into my behavior. Until I was willing to confront my own anger issues and start forgiving and loving myself, I wouldn't be able to fully forgive and love others.

In March of 2001, two years to the month after my mom's passing, I was driving home from work when I noticed the full moon shining brilliantly through the huge oak tree as I pulled into my driveway. I looked up at the sky and became mesmerized by the beauty, grace and love emanating from the full moon.

Intuitively guided to capture this moment, I took a photo of the moon with my 35 mm camera. I was shocked when the photo was developed; the full moon had been transformed into a heart! I truly believe that this was the sign I had been waiting for from Mom.

Mom's sign: The Heart of the Moon.
(Please note: None of the PEP photographs in this book have been altered to create these images.)

---

* Reiki (pronounced Ray-key) is a traditional Japanese technique used for stress reduction to promote wellness of health. Currently there are numerous hospitals, medical clinics and hospice programs incorporating Reiki as a standard part of care.

Chapter 3

"Knowing others is wisdom, knowing yourself is Enlightenment"
Lao-Tzu

A Miraculous Healing

Immediately the tears started and I cried profusely for several minutes. I knew that a profound healing had just happened and it doesn't matter how I knew!

After Mom passed away, I felt a deep void within and a yearning to learn more about nature, healing energy and indigenous wisdom.

One day in April of 2001, while reading a New Age magazine, I saw an article from the Omega Institute offering a week-long course in shape-shifting and shamanism, presented by Dr. Eve Bruce and the Dream Change Coalition, starting in June. They were also offering the opportunity to go to Ecuador in July for two weeks to connect with shamans from both the High Andes and the jungles of the Amazon. My excitement peaked when I read that the trip included a "vision quest" with the sacred medicine plant ayahuasca.

I acted upon the urge to immediately call and register for both the week-long course and the trip to Ecuador. After hanging up the phone, I just knew this was going to be a life-changing experience! Since I knew nothing about the indigenous people of Ecuador and ayahuasca, I began to do extensive research, which heightened my curiosity even more.

I learned, for example, that ayahuasca is called the plant of death and/or rebirth. It is known as a sacred teacher plant that demands respect; and without this respect, it could potentially kill you. Ayahuasca is definitely not a recreational drug. Before you receive its sacred benefits, you must suffer the initial effects: severe vomiting and diarrhea, which seem to clear out toxins in your body.

According to the Wikipedia online encyclopedia, *Aya* in Quechua, the language most widely spoken among the indigenous people of South America, means "spirit" while *huasca* means "vine." I also read that ayahuasca is much—and I emphasize *much*—more powerful than LSD. "What does all this mean?" I recall saying to myself numerous times. "What am I getting myself into? Am I really going to die?"

Some of my friends thought I was nuts, while others encouraged me to follow my intuition and trust that I would have a transformational experience. I knew from deep within that I would have to go beyond my comfort level. I told myself to stop being afraid of feeling that I would crumble, and that even if I lost control, it would be all right.

On the day of my departure, I gave my dogs big hugs goodbye, saying, "I'm leaving for Ecuador for only a few weeks and before you know it, I'll be home!" They probably felt the uncertainty in my voice about knowing exactly who I would be when I returned. With alternating waves of anxiety and high expectations, I kept telling myself, "All is well. I can handle this."

During my flight my eyes were drawn to a cloud mass stretching across the sky: a barrier of some kind. Looking farther out toward the horizon, magnificent shades of deep red, orange and blue colors started to appear. I had the feeling Mother Earth was trying to say,

"See how beautiful I am. Love me instead of destroying me."

I met Dr. Eve Bruce and the rest of the group in Quito, the capital of Ecuador. The next morning at the hotel, we joined in sacred ceremony to bless our journey before traveling by bus to the High Andes to study with the Bird-People shamans known as Yachaks.

Sitting quietly along the way, my thoughts took me back to the springtime when I was diagnosed with hyperplasia of the uterus. It's a condition causing abnormal uterine bleeding and an excessive proliferation of glandular cells, which, in a nutshell, predisposes me to uterine cancer. My doctor recommended hormonal therapy as the treatment of choice. He told me that if hormonal therapy was ineffective I would need a hysterectomy. I didn't like the sound of either option of treatment, but after considerable thought, I decided to try the hormonal therapy. I just wanted the bleeding to stop!

After a few weeks on the hormones I stopped taking them. I didn't like the symptoms I was experiencing: anxiety, frequent headaches and dizziness. When I looked in the Physician Desk Reference book, the authoritative source of FDA-regulated information on prescription drugs, I was shocked to see all of the potential side effects. I called my doctor and I told him I had stopped taking the medication. With great concern in his voice, he instructed me to restart the medication and that if I didn't comply, I would be exposing myself to the need for a hysterectomy.

"Well, the heck with that!" I said in an angry tone. "There must be other options! I'll do some research on alternative therapies when I return from my trip."

I was drawn out of that reflection as we arrived at the Maria Juana Yamberia House of Healing in the valley of Otavalo. Maria Juana Yamberia is a wise, extraordinarily powerful Yachak.

Stepping down from the bus, a group of carefree children of all ages surrounded us and began hugging us. What a wonderful treat to experience these beautiful children hugging us with such open hearts. Looking around, I also felt a powerful energy surrounding us. Encircling this magnificent valley are three sacred, volcanic mountain peaks: Imbabura, Cotocachi and Mojanda. Each one has a specific significance to the Yachak people.

As we entered the healing hut, a short, stocky, bright-eyed, Indian woman arose from her traditional altar in the corner of the room. Dressed in beautifully colored, Quechua clothing and a feathered hat, Maria Juana greeted us with a broad smile radiating from cheek to cheek.

What a powerful presence she possessed! On her altar were sacred stones, called Huacas, gathered from the surrounding volcanoes. Pictures of Jesus and Mary adorned her walls and she shared that they are among the spiritual guides she calls upon to help with her shamanic healing ceremonies. Also in the room was Maria Juana's husband, Antonio, who assists her with the healings. She invited us to sit on the benches lining the two walls and pray. Sitting on a bench close to Maria Juana and her altar, I tried my best to clear my thoughts and just feel the loving energy surrounding us.

In this cultural setting it is the custom to receive healing after taking off your clothes so as to be closer to our natural state. My turn to receive a healing, I stood in the center of the room in front of the group—a humbling experience, yes indeed, but yet quite freeing. This was a great opportunity for me to release all those negative beliefs about my poor body image.

I was given a candle to rub all over my body, and then give it back to Maria Juana to light and examine where the blockages are in my body so she can remove them.

Closing my eyes and allowing myself to surrender, I felt totally safe. Praying, I asked God to please heal me so I can be of greater service to humanity. In the background I vaguely heard chanting to evoke spiritual guidance. After Maria Juana had completed the healing, Antonio guided me back to the bench to quietly dress and sit.

Immediately the tears started and I cried profusely for several minutes. I knew that a profound healing had just happened and it didn't matter how I knew. It was a deep *knowing* within. Turning towards Maria Juana, I felt her immense love and compassion. After each member of our group had received healing, we prepared to leave. I gave Maria Juana a hug *so* tight, not wanting to let her go. I felt so blessed to be in her presence, and I know I will never forget this Earth angel who has committed her life to healing others.

Maria Juana

After my return home, I noticed my uterine bleeding had stopped completely. I knew that Maria Juana and both our angels cured me of hyperplasia. I have learned since that Maria Juana's specialty is treating female reproductive problems. Talk about Divine intervention—how sweet life can be when we trust our intuition!

Chapter 4

"Healing may not be so much about getting better, as about letting go of everything that isn't you – all the expectations, all of the beliefs – and becoming who you are."
Rachel Naomi Remen

Ayahuasca: The Sacred Medicine Plant

Feeling stuck, trapped, and absolutely helpless to escape, I fought the visions endlessly, tossing back and forth on my cot, praying and praying to remove the fear, but to no avail.

One of the places where the sacred healing plant ayahuasca is found is in the upper Amazon basin area of Miazal—home to the Shuar people of Ecuador. The only way to get in and out of this area of the dense green jungle is by small plane, or by foot and canoe, which can take several weeks.

A few days after visiting Maria Juana, we flew there from Quito in a small, single-engine plane with only enough seats for half the group at one time. Landing this plane on a narrow, dirt airstrip is a major challenge. Holding my breath, feeling my stomach fluttering, and hearing the suitcases bouncing around, we landed safely. All six of us commended the pilot on a great job and gave him lots of hugs.

Young, muscular Shuar warriors greeted us and carried our luggage to the river, where we boarded dugout canoes to take us down the mighty Mangosiza River to our Miazal village destination.

Over the next few days, while adjusting to jungle life without Western comforts, we started forming bonds with the Shuar. Proud, kind, sensitive and earth-honoring people, they are true warriors with the reputation of being the only tribe in South America never to be conquered. We had been instructed not to have eye contact with the male Shuar, for if you do, it means you want to have sex with them. I obliged, but found it difficult not to have eye contact because I am used to connecting with people's eyes to see the truth in them.

For the first few days, our group hiked the jungle trails to neighboring villages to listen to the Shuar talk about honoring Mother Earth. Through our interpreter, Juan Gabriel, Eve's assistant, they talk about how to truly thrive in the jungle. "Open your hearts and listen to the plants and animals. They are whispering wisdom into your ears," said a young Shuar warrior.

While walking through the tangled jungle thicket, a light rain began to mist my face. For a fleeting second, I felt my heart connecting to the plant next to me as my soul essence merged with nature. Unfortunately, as soon as my mind or ego became aware of this connection, the feeling would slip away, a very sad moment indeed.

The big day had come. I fasted in preparation to take the sacred plant medicine ayahuasca later on that evening. The previous night, my roommate had taken ayahuasca, and she seemed to have had a quiet, insightful experience—without dying… not *physically* anyway.

Half the group was scheduled to take ayahuasca one night, while the other half was assigned to be individual "buddies" whose task it was to keep a watchful eye for any problems and to help assist our partners to the bathroom in the jungle when necessary.

We all took a long hike while the shaman prepared the ayahuasca, which is an all-day, sacred ceremonial process. Throughout the day I did my best not to focus on the stories I have read on the Internet about ayahuasca, saying to myself, "This is going to be a piece of cake; I can stay in control of this plant."

That evening, we gathered at a traditional Shuar house with a thatched rooftop and a hard-packed dirt floor. Specially modified for Western visitors to commune in and hold healing ceremonies at night, it was called the Round Room and had bamboo slats making up only half of the sidewalls, with the other half of the room wide open to the jungle. A slow-burning fire in the center of the room created the only light source. Three or four hammocks and benches made from old, dugout canoes were placed along the edges of the room. After settling into one of the hammocks, I looked out into the scary, dark jungle. The night air was warm and humid; I couldn't see anything, but I could hear loud, unfamiliar, exotic jungle sounds.

Ayahuasca wrapped around tree.

It came my turn to stand up in front of the shaman to ingest a small cup of ayahuasca and I felt a jolt of anxiety! Standing still and observing every move the shaman made, my heart began to pound like the sound of a beating drum when he made the sign of the cross in front of me as I gulped down the thick, brown, bitter-tasting ayahuasca. I thanked him and slowly returned to my hammock, saying to myself, "Oh my God! He didn't make the sign of the cross for anyone else. I think I am f....ed!"

Shortly after taking this sacred plant medicine, I could hear wretching noises from the people vomiting in the jungle. I kept on saying to myself, "It has been a long while now and nothing is happening to me. Maybe I am so healthy I won't be affected by it." Well, let me tell you… these thoughts were short-lived. I soon felt an uncomfortable sensation in my head and then thought, "Oh my! Here I go! I can't believe I just went past my comfort level."

I remember almost nothing until it was time for me to receive a healing from the shaman. My big buddy who was watching over me asked in a worried tone, "Are you okay?" Not capable of talking, I pushed her away to signal that I didn't want to be touched. I opened my eyes and it was like I was looking through a nearly impenetrable mist, barely able to see anyone. Then I faintly heard Eve and Juan Gabriel come up and say to me, "Diane, let us help you walk to the shaman for your healing." At that point I was physically unable to talk or walk by myself. After some resistance on my part, they picked me up from the hammock and helped me to the bench where the shaman waited, chanting in an ecstatic trance.

The only thing I could barely see through my severely impaired vision was the shaman shaking a bundle of sacred plants all over my body. I vaguely heard him chanting prayers of healing. At the same time he was making sounds of sucking out toxins and negative energies from my body. I had no concept of time or reality, and it didn't matter anyway at this point. I had lost total control of my mind! This was the one thing I had dreaded all my life. I think this is why I have always felt the need to be in control.

After the healing, I was helped to the cot in my small, makeshift bedroom. All of a sudden, I saw in my mind's eye everything, and I mean everything, blowing up: my home, my neighbors, my bills, and then *myself*. When I saw Jesus blow up I became terrified. Saying to myself, "My God, I have died and gone to Hell! The nuns lied to me! I can't believe I am going to be here for eternity!" I felt stuck, trapped, and absolutely helpless to escape. I fought the visions endlessly, tossing back and forth on my cot, praying and praying to remove the fear, but to no avail.

The next thing I realized was Eve, sitting next to me and saying in a soft, muffled tone, "Diane don't fight it. Just relax."

Not knowing where I was in this Godforsaken place in my mind, I heard a crystal-clear Voice speaking to me, "There are no judgments; no right or wrong; no good or bad." As I was hearing the Voice, I saw everything around me continue to blow up. It was like watching a movie that kept going, going and going around. I finally replied to the Voice, "Okay, I get it. Let's move on."

"No, you don't get it my child," said the Voice. Again and again, I would see the same movie and hear the same message. And always I would say, "I get it now," while the Voice continued to emphasize the opposite message and began giving examples of how I was judging people, places and things.

My frustration and mental struggle was now becoming unbearable. I couldn't stop the movie nor the message going through my mind. Also, I was unable to gauge time and felt like I had been watching this movie or vision forever, and would continue to do so for eternity unless something happened. I became conscious of thinking, "Surrender… yes! I will surrender into the moment and allow this. If I have to watch this movie and listen to the same message for eternity, then so be it. I am too exhausted!"

As soon as I uttered the word *surrender*, the movie, the vision and all anxiety melted into peace and contentment. What a tough lesson! All my life I had been placing judgment on people, places and things, while stunting my spiritual growth. As a child I had been programmed to think in terms of good and bad, right and wrong.

Community area for playing and eating.

Today, I am grateful to have experienced ayahuasca, a truly sacred, Amazon medicine plant. This plant helped me to overcome some of my fears, and showed me that judgments don't serve others or myself. In addition, the plant helped me realize I don't always need to be in control. I am so grateful to have received a great healing from the shaman that night. The Shuar have been taught to look past the Western smile and into our hearts. Many of us are unaware of the fire that burns in our heart and the love that we yearn for. Earth-honoring Westerners are encouraged and welcomed by the Shuar—the shamans and elders. They want you to come to the Amazon rainforest to listen and learn the importance of reconnecting with indigenous wisdom, and to learn how to restore the balance within yourself and Mother Nature.

Unfortunately, due to years of deforestation and oil drilling in the Amazon rainforest, the land on which the indigenous people live is becoming uninhabitable. This is heartbreaking, as they are so in touch with Mother Earth.

Missionary Priest, Shuar child, and Diane enjoying precious moments.

There is an important quote from a Shuar elder I would like to share. "My name is Shakaim Mariano Shakai Ijisam Chumpi. I am Shuar. The Shuar have become beggars, begging the mission for food and education, begging visitors for shirts and stupid wristwatches, begging . . . becoming like the others out there who have lost their way!" What a painfully sad message.

For me, I owe my life to the indigenous people, the shamans and this experience of healing that I have just shared with you. I am doing my best to be a voice for Mother Earth and I hope this resonates with you.

As I write this book, I am continually touched by and feel very blessed to have met and connected with so many Earth-honoring people. I become teary-eyed with the realization that there is a Divine Force protecting and guiding me every step of the way toward self-realization.

Chapter 5

"Trusting in the messages and signs from God is the key to my inner peace."
Heart Moon

The Calling

"Sign number three. I guess I'm going to Costa Rica!"

It was December of 2002 when I read about a weeklong shamanism workshop in Costa Rica, offered by Sandra Ingerman, an internationally-known, shamanic teacher and bestselling author. I felt a strong desire to attend it, in spite of certain dilemmas in my life that were making me question even the possibility of attending.

The previous June, I had decided to sell my home, since I had lived in New Jersey most of my life, and I was feeling the need to close one chapter and begin another. A few hours after setting this intention, I met a couple walking up the private road where I lived. After introducing themselves, they asked, "We are looking to buy a house in this area; do you know of one?" Without hesitation I joyfully exclaimed, "I'm selling my house!"

With happy response, they asked if they could see it, and to make a long story short, they eventually offered to buy my home.

By mid-December I was still anxiously awaiting the closing on the house sale. Thinking about the workshop I wanted to attend, I asked myself, "What if the final closing date on my house happens during the week of the workshop? I've been eagerly awaiting this date since last June and I can't afford to miss any closing responsibilities for the house sale."

Furthermore, I had spent a ton of money over the past two years traveling around the world, and I just couldn't justify spending more until after my home was sold. I decided to ask for Divine Guidance and open myself to receiving a sign whether or not to go.

Later that month, a friend said to me out of the clear blue sky, "Diane, you love nature so much, why not check out Costa Rica? The rainforest and landscape there are simply magnificent." Shocked at what I was hearing, I asked, "Did you say Costa Rica?"

"Yes," he answered in a puzzled tone.

Still somewhat skeptical, I asked for more signs from God whether or not to go, but these requests went unanswered for the time being.

Then, a few weeks later in January, while again talking about my recent travels with a neighbor, he said, "I lived in Costa Rica for a few years. It is a great place to live." Oh my! Costa Rica was coming up again. I hadn't even mentioned that I was thinking about going there. I said still another prayer, petitioning God to give two more signs that day if it was really in my highest interest to attend the workshop. (I had remembered reading that it is important when petitioning God to be specific and include a time frame.)

So I shared my dilemma with some of the nurses at work, telling them that I had petitioned God for two more signs. "Really," they said. Feeling like they might think I was a bit weird, I dropped the subject. Then, about an hour after starting our shift, one of the nurses offered to make me a cup of coffee. "Sure," I said. All of a sudden, she exclaimed in a high-pitched voice, "Oh my God! Guess where the coffee comes from? Costa Rica!"

Hurray! Sign number two.

Later on in my shift, I got a call from the ER (emergency room), informing me about a new admission. The nurse gave me the new patient's report and, for some strange reason, I asked where the patient was from.

"Let me see," said the ER nurse. "From Costa Rica."

"Sign number three. I guess I'm going to Costa Rica!"

My co-workers were just as surprised as I was when I told them. As a result, I began to honor the messages and signs from God, to trust the process and know that it will all turn out fine.

The next morning, I went to Sandra's website (www.sandraingerman.com) and finalized arrangements to attend the workshop, including buying her bestselling book, *Soul Retrieval*.

I had an intuitive *knowing* that this experience was going to be extra special and magical.

The third sign leads the way.

Chapter 6

"Follow your bliss and the Universe will open doors where there were only walls."
Joseph Campbell

A Mystical Encounter in Montezuma

All of a sudden I felt an unusual sensation inside the bottom of my feet—a feeling I had never felt before. And then, without realizing what I was thinking, I heard myself say, "Oh Jesus, please hold my hand."

After receiving all those signs from God about attending the shamanism workshop in Costa Rica, I felt my course was set. When I checked in for my trip at Newark International Airport, I was surprised to have been upgraded to first class. Without question, I accepted this as another unexpected gift, and I began to profusely and joyfully thank God for it.

The flight was very long but I enjoyed traveling in first class immensely. I arrived late at night on February 1st in the Costa Rican capital of San Jose and was transported to the retreat center a few hours away. The next morning I was pleased to meet Sandra Ingerman, especially since I had finished reading her book *Soul Retrieval* and was quite impressed with her expertise on this topic.

After class I mustered up enough courage to ask her if she would be willing to do a soul retrieval on me. I felt I had fragmented parts of my soul that needed healing, particularly from trauma I had experienced as a child. Sandra said, "I will get back to you."

The next day she told me, "There have been many requests for individual soul retrievals, and due to the time constraints, I will not be scheduling individual sessions." In a disappointed tone I replied, "I completely understand."

Costa Rica's pristine virgin rainforest teemed with rare, colorful wildlife. We were offered a variety of activities with opportunities to explore it. A group of us, including Sandra, chose to go whitewater rafting down the Sarapiqué River.

"Today, the rapids are very strong, with a rating of class three," announced our guide. Never having been whitewater rafting before, I was a little nervous but hopeful that we'd be in for a thrilling ride. We received safety instructions, vests and helmets; each raft had an expert guide to help us navigate.

Once on the river, we were immediately greeted with many wild and wet moments as we soared through the rapids. In the brilliant sunlight, the white water literally sparkled. I was having so much fun, I forgot to be afraid. I could faintly hear monkeys, macaws, and toucans singing high above the canopy as we raced down the river.

Suddenly our guide instructed, in a loud, serious voice, "Paddle hard, and fast! Now!" I saw that we had turned toward the bank of the river. We paddled and paddled as fast as we could, but the raft in front of us flipped over and it looked

Flying down the rapids.

like we were going to be next! Suddenly it happened. I was churning deep underwater and I began to panic. People from my raft were on top of me as I desperately tried to push them off, kicking and flailing. If I don't get to the surface quickly, I am going to die, I thought! Somehow we all surfaced, gasping for precious breath. No one was seriously hurt—not physically anyway. Emotionally, however, I felt tremendously traumatized. I suddenly flashed back to when I almost drowned as a small child.

The next morning in class, Sandra invited any of the participants still feeling distressed from yesterday's adventure, to come into the circle and receive a soul retrieval specifically related to the rafting incident. She explained that when we experience any kind of trauma, parts of our essence or soul become fragmented, leaving us feeling unbalanced. The sooner we can bring the body back into harmony, the better, which the technique of soul retrieval is able to do.

I stepped into the circle and looked around, surprised that I'm the only one there. Sandra asked me to lie down so my body could feel calm and relaxed.

Lying on the floor, I felt a tremendous amount of support and love from the group. I tried not to think, but rather to just focus on feeling the energy. When Sandra had completed the soul retrieval, she told me she was instructed by her helper spirits to retrieve not only the fragmented parts of yesterday's rafting incident, but also to retrieve parts of my soul that were traumatized when I was a child. Hearing the word *child*, I felt deep within me a profound sense of gratitude and oneness. Sandra and I immediately hugged and cried together. It was a moment I will never forget; a powerful healing had taken place deep inside.

What I find incredible is that in order to have a soul retrieval experience that helped heal my inner childhood trauma, I needed to experience the rafting incident. Little Diane was very grateful. How wonderful to have had a soul retrieval with a world-renowned expert!

This incident has deepened my trust in the Divine. I'm learning that I can gain great wisdom and knowledge through such spiritually guided events. Although remaining calm when faced with impending death is not an easy task, the rafting episode also taught me not to panic when confronted with unexpected, frightening situations.

Later on that week we paired up with a partner to help gain a deeper connection with our helper spirits. At the end of the exercise, my partner told me that her helper spirit suggested I learn more about the Goddess Kuan Yin. The goddess of compassion and love, she told me, Kuan Yin protects women and children. Saying to myself, "Oh, okay. I will store her in my memory bank and someday check her out." I had no idea how important Kuan Yin would be to me later on in life.

When I booked my Costa Rica workshop, I had made plans to stay an extra few days somewhere else, but up to this point I did not know where. Again, I decide to trust my intuition to lead me to where I would be staying next. Nearing the end of the workshop, I was getting a little nervous thinking that my plans to travel to another part of the country were not coming together as well as I had expected. Later, a Reiki practitioner who works at the retreat center suggested traveling to the small Costa Rican village of Montezuma on the southern tip of the Nicoya Peninsula.

Enthusiastically she said, "There is a bed and breakfast there that you would love, Diane, and it is close to the ocean." I paused for a moment and then said, "It sounds like a great plan."

I immediately made reservations with Sansa Airlines and arranged for a taxi on arrival at Playa Tambor Airport for transport to the village of Montezuma. (Playa Tambor is referred to locally as "Whale Bay.") Making reservations for the first evening at the recommended bed and breakfast, I was pleasantly surprised to see all my plans come together in less than an hour. All I can say is, "Hurray!"

It's only a 25-minute flight to the small and rugged Tambor airstrip. As the one-engine plane was about to land, I became anxious. Grateful and relieved to see the taxi driver waiting for me, I learned that he spoke a little English and knew where the bed and breakfast was located, a definite plus. Driving on winding roads covered with dust and huge potholes filled with muddy water, we finally arrived at the B&B, just outside of Montezuma. In awe seeing the picturesque jungle beach a few miles down the mountain, I reflect back to what my friend back home in New Jersey had said when he told me that I would love Costa Rica. He was absolutely right on!

Greeted with open arms by the two women who own the B&B, I had a tour of the rooms and walked around to the back of the house, where I saw a huge, well-constructed stone labyrinth. Oh, how I love walking and meditating in labyrinths. I found this place quite enchanting but I was very disappointed to hear the beach was a 45-minute walk away. Of course I knew it would take me another 45 minutes or more to walk back up. After a day in the sun, this walk would be grueling. A little voice in my head said, "Don't settle for less!"

I asked if there were any hotels closer to the beach. One of the owners was very helpful and helped me find a private room with a shared bath right on the beach. "Perfect!" I exclaimed. She graciously called for a taxi and, apologizing for their inconvenience, I thanked them and off I went.

Kuan Yin in the entrance hallway of the hotel.

Within ten minutes I was dropped off at the hotel, where I was pleased to see stunning, ocean views. Walking through to the reception area, I spotted a statue and asked, "Who is this?" I was shocked when I heard, "Kuan Yin."

"Kuan Yin!' I said in a loud baffled tone, "the Chinese goddess of compassion and healing who protects women and children?"

"Yes," she says in a calm, contemplative voice.

A whopping "*Wow*" was my response.

To walk into a Costa Rican hotel in a primarily Christian-based country and find a Kuan Yin statue is not an everyday occurrence. I felt truly blessed, divinely guided and honored.

The days that followed were filled with exploring the quaint, small village of Montezuma and the surrounding jungle filled with waterfalls and exquisite wildlife. At night my senses were stimulated by the loud, howling sounds coming from the Howler Monkeys in the jungle nearby.

Howler Monkey singing in the canopy.

On the morning of February 11th, the day I was leaving Montezuma, I wanted to take advantage of the few hours left by soaking up the sun and gazing at the extraordinarily, crystal clear ocean water. I settled into a hammock behind the hotel.

All of a sudden, the wind kicked up and I started to feel an unusual sensation inside the bottom of my feet—a feeling I had never felt before. And then, without realizing what I was thinking, I heard myself say, "Oh Jesus, please hold my hand." The intense pulsing sensation moved quickly up and down my body twice. I had absolutely no recollection of time nor space for the next few hours. When I awoke and looked at my watch, I had just enough time to pack and be ready for the taxi to take me to the airstrip.

On the way back home to New Jersey, I pondered my recent experiences. Wondering about the intense pulsing sensation I experienced on the last morning in Costa Rica, I believe I received a Divine healing. Back in 1998, when I was experiencing the dark night of my soul, I recalled asking God, "Please heal me, so I may be of greater service to humanity."

Chapter 7

"You must be the change you wish to see in the world"
Mohandas K. Gandhi

Farewell New Jersey

And what is most important to me, and what nobody can ever forget once seen, are the dolphins and whales.

I can identify the defining point in my journey of self-discovery as 13 years ago. This meant addressing issues in my past that were not so pleasant: shame, guilt, low self-worth and the big "R"—*Resentments* (especially toward my family). Once I started resolving these issues on a deeper level, I was beginning to feel more of a sense of self-empowerment and freedom in my daily life.

As a result, there was nothing holding me back from leaving New Jersey. The commitment to take care of my mother had been fulfilled. It was time to move on to uncharted waters and start my new life.

Walking outside, past the lovely rock gardens that I built, I began to seriously contemplate life questions such as, "Where would I like to live? Since I have a degree in nursing I can probably move anywhere, well…almost anywhere." I sat on one of the rocks in the brook that ran through my property and turned my attention to the babbling water flowing effortlessly around me.

An intriguing thought popped into my head. "Where would I like my dream home to be?" Immediately, I visualized living in a warm, tropical place, close to the water, among trees and within a community that honors Mother Earth. After saying a little prayer for guidance, two places came to mind: New Mexico and Hawaii. With enthusiasm, I said to myself, "Okay, I'll travel to both and see which one feels like home!"

A view of Diane's backyard.

After spending two wonderful weeks in New Mexico, I decided it didn't quite feel like home. Telling myself it was time to explore Hawaii, I just happened to have the opportunity to take a workshop about Hawaiian spirituality on the island of Kauai. So I made all the necessary reservations and called a friend to take care of my dogs and house sit for two weeks.

During the workshop, I had visions about going to Molokai. Again, not questioning the guidance, after the workshop I spent two glorious, unforgettable days on the island of Molokai.

One of the seven major Hawaiian islands, Molokai is often called the "Friendly Isle." For others, as well as for me, this place is like stepping back in time about 50 years. There are no traffic lights or malls and the buildings are no taller than a palm tree. Glamorous it's not, but brilliantly natural it is! What I find so appealing about Molokai is its spectacular, raw beauty, and the local hospitality bursting with the Hawaiian spirit. It is such a relaxing, "to die for" place. Life is slow, laid back, tropical, rural and, most of all, peaceful—something I deeply desired in my life.

In the middle of the Pacific Ocean, 2,300 miles from the nearest land mass, I fell in love with Hawaii. Its rainforests, unspoiled, white-sand beaches, and clean, warm, ocean water, teeming with vibrant life, enchanted me. What is ultimately most important to me, and what nobody can ever forget once seen, are the dolphins and whales. Hawaii embraced my heart with her Aloha spirit.

Without a doubt in my mind now, and with a big smile on my face, I announced jubilantly, "I am ready to say goodbye to New Jersey and my past! Hawaii, here I come!"

Into the unknown with grace and ease.

Chapter 8

"Ask questions from your heart and you will be answered from the heart."
Omaha Proverb

Moving to Hawaii: Crossing the Threshold

I immediately start to cry and can't stop. My body begins to shake violently as the emotional pain pours out.

The closing on my house was at long last finalized. The only difficult things to leave behind were some family, close friends, and my two beloved dogs. The quarantine period for dogs coming to Hawaii is three months, and I couldn't imagine them locked up that long. I made the painful decision to leave my two very special dogs, Delia and Peaches, behind with my nephew and a close friend.

On March 3, 2003, I began a long, grueling, 3,000-plus mile drive across the continental United States to California, where I dropped off my car at the designated pier in Oakland to be shipped to Honolulu. Finally, stepping aboard the plane and seating myself, I took a deep breath and said quietly to myself with a great big smile, "Destination…Paradise!"

During the next seven months, while living on the island of Oahu, I found my yearning for travel and adventure not yet satisfied. Oahu is considered the "Gathering Place," and for me, its multi-cultural character was a hub with spokes leading out to people and places I had yet to explore.

I was first inspired to travel to Brazil and spent a week with a man called "John of God" (a dedicated, powerful Brazilian healer), and a week with Sandra Ingerman to participate in her "Medicine for the Earth" teacher training workshop.

Driving towards Uluru.

I also took a trip to Australia to spend six courageous weeks connecting with and learning about the Aboriginal culture. I rented a monster of a four-wheel-drive vehicle to take me into the more remote regions known as *The Bush*. From Alice Springs, I drove to Uluru (the official Aboriginal name), also known as Ayers Rock, a mysterious, prehistoric site that is approximately 200 million years old.

This land and rock is sacred to the aboriginal people and is recognized as a World Heritage Area for both its natural and cultural value. I was inspired by the immense natural beauty and powerful energy surrounding the rock, and I took a photograph that revealed a ball of Light—an unexplained phenomenon "PEP", and I view it as a sphere of pure Divine Love.

Looking in my viewfinder, I am astounded to see a PEP appearing as a perfectly pure, white sphere of Light.

While sitting on the rock meditating, I felt an energetic presence surround me and say, "Move to Hilo and you will be taken care of." At first I thought, "I don't want to move to Hilo on the Big Island of Hawaii. It rains there all the time!" But after some reflection, and remembering how I had trusted that inner Voice, I decided to pay closer attention to what I just heard.

I was grateful for having had the opportunity to visit Brazil and Australia. Both those countries and the people have *immensely* enriched my spiritual development. While flying back to Oahu, and still thinking about the guidance I received in Australia, I made plans to relocate to Hilo. My plans fell easily and effortlessly into place. It was late October 2003, and I located an inexpensive, three-bedroom condominium with gorgeous views of the Wainaku River flowing into Hilo Bay. "Ah," I whispered to myself, "I guess this is part of the "you will be taken care of" message."

A few months later, while reading an article about the World Indigenous Peoples gathering of local and global healing, presented by Tutu Emma Kaahuhailikaukoalaa Foundation, my interest was aroused when suddenly I felt a sharp pain in my big toe. I had by then become accustomed to knowing when my intuition wants my attention. I get physical sensations like goose pumps, locally known as *chicken skin*, and when it is really important, sharp pains occur in my big toe. The pain immediately goes away when I affirm to myself, "Okay, I'll check this out," or something similar.

This was a weeklong retreat called "Awaken the Dynamic Power of Healing, Unconditional Love and the Light of Lokahi Deep Within." Going to the website to find out all the details, including cost, I did a double take. "Wow, over $3,000! Am I nuts? I just spent a fortune traveling to Australia this past month and now, with the move and having to buy furniture for my condo, I'd better think twice about this!" Then, my very next thought was, "Oh well, the heck with the money. I'm just going to trust my intuition."

During the very first day of the retreat, I intuitively heard, "Just shine your Light. You don't have to do anything else." With confidence I say, "No problem, I can do that."

By the third day, it was becoming increasingly difficult to just "be" and shine my Light. I was starting to judge and criticize our facilitator. Becoming more and more intolerant, I thought, "She is always so late for our group meetings, and…talk about being disorganized! We don't know what we're doing from one minute to the next."

Fueling my anger and frustration, the rest of the group was also feeling the same way and I began to believe that I had placed way too many expectations on this gathering. I didn't make a connection with the lessons learned years ago in Ecuador from the master medicine plant ayahuasca. Once again…deep within…I hear, "Just shine your Light." And again my mind tells me, "I can't do it!"

My judgments were snowballing into resentment and preventing the Light from shining through. At the same time, I began to realize that my feelings were also becoming toxic to others as well as to myself. Knowing from experience how important it is to acknowledge my feelings, I decided to muster up the courage to talk to the co-facilitator. "I am very angry and frustrated," I said. "I spent a lot of money to attend this gathering, and I am now wondering if I made the correct decision."

He listened politely to me going on and on without judging me, and then helped me explore my childhood feelings of fear and lack. I shared vivid memories with him of being violated and betrayed by family members while I yearned for their acceptance, nurturing and love. I know my parents loved me, but I didn't feel their love a lot of the time while I was growing up. The co-facilitator helped me release toxic emotions that didn't serve me anymore and I began to feel much freer.

The next day, during one of our group sessions, I asked our facilitator to forgive me for judging her. Immediately I started to cry and couldn't stop—my body shaking violently as the emotional pain poured out. At the same time, I also asked my inner child for forgiveness. The facilitator came over and held me tightly. In native Hawaiian traditions, the process of resolving conflict through forgiveness and love is called *ho'oponopono*.

A few days after this experience, I scheduled a healing session with one of the participants, an Australian massage therapist and energy healer. I felt that she was genuine and had my highest interest at heart.

While lying on my back on the massage table, I breathed deeply to stop the chatter in my mind. As she gently rocked my head back and forth, I said a prayer of intention to receive clarity about my life and the gathering I was attending. I again questioned the visions I was receiving. "Am I making all this up? Is it just my imagination?" Reminding myself that I did indeed ask to receive messages and visions for my highest good, I answered myself, "Why ask, if I am not going to trust what I see and hear?"

Toward the end of the session I felt my crown chakra (the energy center at the top of my head) open and expand outwardly. Taking long deep breaths from my *pico* (abdomen), I felt Divine Light flowing in and entering my heart. The vision I saw is a pure, white ball of love penetrating my heart and expanding blissfully throughout every cell of my body. Next came the message, "Shine your Light. If you forget, remember this image."

The image was the photograph I took at Uluru (Ayers Rock), Australia in September 2003—the ball of white Light that I view as a sphere of pure Divine Love.

Slowly I was realizing that I create every facet of my reality in conjunction with the Universe and Divine Guidance, in order to teach me lessons I came here to learn.

From this wonderful vision and message, I hold in my heart many insights that I'd like to share with you, too:

• To shine my Light brightly, I need to release and let go of judgments toward others and myself.

• Living in the moment requires patience.

• I need to have respect and compassion for another's journey, even if it is very different from my own.

From lessons learned throughout this chapter of my life, I became more inspired to embark on a special voyage exploring more unusual light phenomena. It's a pathway I take by following my intuition and, along the way, learning a lot more about myself on this adventurous, cosmic journey.

Let Love lead the way!

Chapter 9

"We must learn to reawaken and keep ourselves awake; not by mechanical aid, but by an infinite expectation of the dawn."
                                    Henry David Thoreau

The Photographic Energy Phenomena

"Oh my God! Wow!" I was stunned to see the photo of Lono with the PEP wrapped around him.

Upon arising one morning, I looked out over the *lanai* (porch) of my condo and saw a large sea turtle swimming down the peaceful Wainaku River. "What a brilliant day for an adventure exploring the other side of the Big Island," I thought. The sky was clear blue and the sun just coming up over the horizon.

After breakfast, a warm shower and a short meditation, I gathered up some road-trip snacks and hopped into my Subaru with a sense of excitement in my blood. "Which route shall I take?" I asked of my guardian angels.

Knowing it takes about two hours on either road, I decided to take the southern route to the western side of the island. It passes through Hawaii Volcanoes National Park, which contains two of the most active volcanoes in the world: Kilauea and Mauna Loa. Driving along Highway 11, I began to feel an unfamiliar energy sensation in my body. "I wonder what this feeling is?" I asked out loud to no one in particular.

Hot lava flowing into the ocean producing intense heat and steam.

According to traditional Hawaiian legend, Pele… Goddess of fire, volcanoes, lightning and creation lives in Kilauea. Many people believe in this and have had encounters with her intense creative energy in the Hawaiian Islands. Pele's fiery passion ignites my own creative energy as well. I have had many opportunities to see boiling, glowing, molten lava cascading down the mountain and pouring over the cliff into the ocean—an unforgettable, energizing experience!

After passing the park and making a few stops to gaze at the breathtaking, mighty surf along the southern coastline, I saw a sign for Pu'uhonua o Honaunau National Park. Being an inquisitive explorer, I turned onto Ke Ala o Keawe, the road leading to the entrance to the shoreline park. Getting out of my car, I got a distinct feeling that this place is both sacred and enchanting.

The park ranger there explained that the name Pu'uhonua o Honaunau translates as the Place of Refuge at Honaunau. It was a sanctuary where those who had broken the king's strict, sacred laws or *kapu* could be forgiven… provided they survived the treacherous swim across shark-infested Honaunau Bay. The high priest, or *kahuna*, would perform a cleansing ritual, absolving the person of any wrongdoing. This provided a second chance for Hawaiian people who had been sentenced to death.

Meandering the guided path, I explored this huge, historic cultural site, admired the tall, majestic Royal Palm trees blowing calmly in the wind and was awestruck at the expansive, jagged, black lava field jutting out to sea. It is truly an exquisite sight.

The entrance view of the Place of Refuge.

A carved "tiki" just inside the park entrance caught my eye. This medium size figure with piercing eyes and a menacing grin startled me at first, even though this is not the first time I've seen tiki statues. Many indigenous cultures from around the world use them in religious or spiritual ceremonies and practices.

According to the Wikipedia definition, tiki "refer to large wood and stone carvings of humanoid forms…which serve to mark the boundaries of sacred sites."

This particular tiki depicts one of the four major Hawaiian gods—Lono, who was the god of fertility and peace. According to the ranger, tiki statues were placed strategically around this park to ward off unwanted, harmful energy or spirits. Lono was, and still is, revered by many Hawaiians.

As the sun was starting to set over the ocean, I took out my camera and began taking photographs of an imposing sunset. Before dark, I also photographed the surrounding thatched huts, the Great Wall and the Lono tiki. It wasn't until the next day, back in Hilo, bright-eyed and ready to start my day, I downloaded the photographs.

"Oh my God, Wow!" I was stunned to see the photo of Lono with the PEP wrapped around him. It was truly an unexpected gift from Pu'uhonua o Honaunau.

PEP wrapped around the Tiki Lono.

After my experience at the Place of Refuge, I began to examine my photos more closely and often spotted these white—sometimes colored—balls, plasma fields, filaments and unique, well-defined, cloud formations. Always skeptical, I considered it might be dust, sun flares or other camera aberrations causing these phenomena. I even tried using different cameras, but continued to get the same results. Interestingly though, whenever I took a second photo at the same site immediately after the shot containing a PEP, the phenomena are either no longer present, or they have move to a different area of the scene.

Looking back on photos I've taken previously, I was astounded to realize they'd been appearing for some time now. In a baffled tone I asked, "Why are you showing up at certain times and places and why are you appearing in my photo shots?"

Researching the Internet in 2004, I soon discovered there wasn't much information available regarding these apparitions. By 2010, however, more and more people were reporting unexplainable, round shapes, often termed "energy orbs," showing up in their photos.

I believe these PEP are energies of Light vibrating at different frequencies, as evidenced by their unique shapes and colors. Realizing the importance of differentiating between the explainable and unexplainable, I decided to enroll in photography classes to expand my skills and see if there is any logical explanation why colored balls and filaments are showing up in the photos. To my surprise there isn't. Although the teacher emphasized the importance of being able to differentiate between sun flares, camera aberrations and the PEP, he agreed with me that the PEP are unexplainable and quite unique—not the result of any camera aberration. Nevertheless, I emphasize that I'm not a professional photographer; I'm just sharing my personal experiences and insights about the PEP.

When I'm feeling intuitively guided to take a photo and see PEP in my viewfinder, I immediately take another one. If the PEP has disappeared or moved, I'm confident it is PEP. If I don't see any movement, I'm inclined to think it's not PEP.

For example, I took a photograph of the full moon on December 31, 2009, with my Canon 5D. When I looked into my viewfinder and saw a blue ball of light, I was thrilled, thinking I had captured PEP. I continued to photograph the blue ball, which appeared to be moving around the moon. I didn't realize at the time that I also was moving, which created the *illusion* that the blue ball was moving. I thought I had photographed the most mystical photo of all time, especially since the blue ball was appearing around not just a full moon but also a "blue moon" (a rare occurrence of two full moons within the same month). When the blue ball showed up again while photographing another full moon on November 20th, 2010, I became suspicious. This time I remained perfectly still and so did the blue ball of light. I took many photos of the moon that night and the blue ball always remained stationary.

Blue ball of light during the full moon.
(Once in a Blue Moon.)

After taking a second photo it appears
the blue ball moved but it didn't. I moved.

A close-up view of the Blue Moon.

The full moon on 11-20-2010. The ball of light remained stationary after taking a second photo.

Not sure if the blue ball of light was a camera aberration or PEP, I went to a camera shop and showed one of the camera experts my blue-ball-of-light photos. I learned that most likely the blue ball was a mirror reflection of the full moon and that the sensor in my camera created the blue color. Even though I was a little disappointed that the blue ball of light wasn't a mystical, loving PEP, the explanation seemed logical and correct.

I tell you this to help you realize that I am a seeker of my own truth and that I am gaining greater insights and wisdom every day. Integrity and honesty are two of the most important keys for truly awakening my authentic self.

I encourage the reader to have fun and look back on photos you have taken, and examine them closely. There just may be PEP hidden there, as a loving Divine Presence that will connect to your heart and offer you some needed guidance and wisdom. To me, these PEP energies in the photos are not threatening. I believe they are "energies of love" and I feel honored to be associated with them.

Female hula dancer with a PEP on her head. I spoke to the male hula dancer at this Luau I attended. After I showed him this photo with the PEP he said, "Oh, that must be my ancestors watching over me."

I was intuitively guided to go to St. Augustine Catholic Church in Waikiki, Hawaii, to photograph this tree next to the entrance of the church. After seeing the large PEP in my first photo, I immediately took another. The large PEP had relocated to the left of the tree.

Close-up view.

Seeking more of my own truth, I would find time in the next two weeks to go back to Pu'uhonua o Honaunau and meditate at the tiki of Lono.

Chapter 10

*"My family is not confined to mother, mate, and child;
but it includes all creatures be they tame or wild."*
Alice S. Carpenter

The Dolphins' Loving Presence

After about an hour, I emerged from the water feeling rejuvenated and whispered to myself, "The water really wasn't that cold!"

A few weeks later, I traveled back to Pu'uhonua o Honaunau, hoping to receive some insight regarding the PEP wrapped around the Lono tiki in my photo. It was a late Saturday afternoon and I sat down next to tiki of Lono, saying, "I'm prepared as well as determined to sit next to you all night, if necessary, and get some answers."

Around 7:30 p.m. it started to rain. "Now what?" I thought. "I don't want to sit here in the rain and get soaked all night!" Disappointed at not receiving any insight over the past few hours, I packed up my chair and headed back to the car.

I decided to drive a short distance away to another part of Honaunau Bay, where I notice a local Hawaiian keeping a watchful eye for any trespassers at night. I asked, "Can I sleep in my car here tonight?" His initial answer was no, but after telling him my story, he answered in a fatherly tone, "Okay, I will watch over you."

Thankful and relieved, I settled into the back seat of my car; I focused my attention on the soothing sounds of the ocean and eventually fell asleep.

Awakening the next morning around 5 a.m., I saw my new Hawaiian friend sitting on a bench nearby and asked, "Do you see any dolphins?"

"Not yet," he tells me.

At the bench where he is sitting, I gave him a huge hug in gratitude for watching out for me during the night. I left and drove the five or six miles to Kealakekua Bay to look for the dolphins. When I arrived I was excited to see a pod of dolphins and a few early-morning dolphin lovers swimming together. Somewhat reticently, I wondered, "Do I really want to get into the water this early in the morning? It has to be ice cold!"

I casually ask someone I saw entering into the water, "Is the water cold?"

He yelled back in a confident tone, "Not too bad. It will warm up as the sun comes over the mountain."

Still hesitating, I immediately heard my intuition speak to me: "Don't be a wimp! You'll have fun swimming with the dolphins." I *am* a wimp when it comes to feeling the cold, which helps explain why I relocated to the tropical state of Hawaii from New Jersey!

Mustering up enough courage, I stepped in and swam out to the dolphins. Wow, what an experience! The spinner dolphins swam playfully all around me! I felt like I had died and gone to heaven! For some mystical reason, dolphins have an amazing ability to transmit to us such joy and happiness.

After about an hour, I emerged from the water feeling rejuvenated and whispered to myself, "The water really wasn't that cold!" I was really proud of myself for having gone beyond my comfort level to experience the magic of playing with these majestic beings of the sea. Slowly and blissfully, I walked to the restroom and changed into shorts and a T-shirt.

Still determined to receive some insight, I drove back to Pu'uhonua o Honaunau. Entering the park around 8 a.m., I walked back to the tiki Lono and again sat next to him. Somewhat relieved that no one else was around, I set an intention and said a prayer to receive wisdom and insight.

An hour or so later, I heard intuitively, "Yes, this place is still very sacred and what you have captured in the photograph is spiritual healing energy." Taking a moment to allow these words to flow into my heart space, I felt the truth in this message. With a heartfelt prayer of deep gratitude, I left and drove home to Hilo.

Many years later, I now live on the west side of this island and have become a frequent visitor to the Place of Refuge. One afternoon I decided to take a walk on the beach. This was soon after talking to one of my closest friends on the telephone sharing doubts about my writing abilities and other self-limiting thoughts I had about completing this book. Instead of walking to the closest beach, which is just a block from my home, I decided to drive to Pu'uhonua o Honaunau.

Walking around in the park, I noticed a Hawaiian man carving a tiki. After introducing myself, I told him about the spiritual healing energy photographs I've taken and the book I am writing. Initially, Charlie, also known as Kale in Hawaiian, seemed aloof and uninterested. I realize that Kale sees hundreds of tourists a week in the National Heritage Site, with many asking the same questions about what he is carving. Sending him loving Light, I continued to talk to him about the Photographic Energy Phenomena I am capturing with my camera. After a short while, he moved closer to me and gazed intently into my eyes. Within moments, Kale began to speak freely about his ancestors, who date back many generations here on the Big Island. He confirmed my belief that this place is truly a sacred sanctuary of peaceful, healing energy for people to come and receive. He then advised me that this unusual energy phenomenon is coming to me for a specific purpose and strongly encouraged me to continue writing this book. "Not everyone is gifted with taking these types of photos," he told me with a firm voice.

We hugged goodbye in the traditional Hawaiian way: nose-to-nose, forehead-to-forehead. I walked away feeling tremendously inspired to continue writing *Intuitive Adventures beyond the Camera Lens*.

I believe God speaks through people, and Kale was *certainly* one of those people. As I am writing this chapter, I hear God say, "Diane, you're doing great, keep writing and following your intuition!"

Hawaiian Spinner Dolphins having an intimate moment.

Chapter 11

*"Isn't it wonderful that all Beings of Light, whether human or animal,
are responding to the Universe's call to care for us."*

Heart Moon

The Horse with No Name

Checking the viewfinder, I was awe-struck when I saw a PEP on the mane of the horse resting its head on my car.

Heartfelt experiences are very special to me, so I would like to share with you two very memorable occasions. The first one occurred while living in Hilo on the Big Island of Hawaii, the second one with my family in New Jersey.

After attending an intensive weekend workshop learning the art of Qigong* in Hawi, on the northern part of the Big Island, I was feeling a bit lonely and decided to stop by my favorite horse ranch on the way home. Stepping out of the car and looking around, I saw a herd of horses a short distance away in the pasture.

I closed my eyes and opened my heart, asking the horses if they'd like to come and say "Hi." Slowly opening my eyes, I was awestruck to see four horses closely surrounding my car. The loneliness had completely disappeared and I felt waves of love pulsating throughout my body. There is not a word in the dictionary to describe the immense gratitude I felt for these majestic Beings of Light!

A heartfelt embrace.

---

* "Qigong (or ch'i kung) refers to a wide variety of traditional cultivation practices that involve methods of accumulating, circulating, and working with qi, breathing or energy within the body. Qigong is practiced for health maintenance purposes, as a therapeutic intervention, as a medical profession, a spiritual path and/or component of Chinese arts." This information is from Wikipedia online encyclopedia.

Regaining my conscious awareness, so to speak, I pulled out my camera and took some photographs of this very blissful moment. Checking the viewfinder, I was awe-struck when I saw a PEP on the mane of the horse resting its head on my car!

Isn't it wonderful that all Beings of Light, whether human or animal, are responding to the Universe's call to care for us!

The "Horse With No Name." with a PEP on his mane.

A second extraordinarily heartfelt experience occurred while spending precious moments with my family. We were talking about Mom, who had transitioned into Heaven on March 3rd, 1999, when I took this photo on May 18th, 2007.

Visiting family and sharing memorial moments about Mom.

A PEP appears while talking about my mom. The dog in the photo is one of my animal angels, Delia.

Following an intuitive urge to take another photograph just 30 seconds after the first. I captured something I can't prove, but I believe with all my heart that the PEP on the stairs is Mom revealing herself in a loving and unfamiliar way. I believe, when we really take the time to be aware of what is happening around us and seize the moment to observe nature, we can make intriguing discoveries of phenomena like the PEP. They are revealing themselves to let us know we are *not alone* in this world, and they are messengers of love.

Chapter 12

"Love All, Serve All. Help Ever, Hurt Never."
Sai Baba

Return to India

"Go to India in two weeks for a healing."

In Mid-March of 2004 I had just completed an intense Kundalini yoga practice, and I had a vision of Sai Baba, as clear as day, speaking these words through my "third-eye vision," "Go to India in two weeks for a healing."

Sai Baba's words definitely got my attention as I felt the powerful need to return to India. I exclaimed loudly to God, "I don't want to go to India again! I'm not a devotee of Sai Baba and I don't even know where his ashrams are! India is not an easy place to visit, you know!"

According to Lonely Planet's Internet website, India is described as: *"Bamboozling.* There's simply no other word that convincingly captures the enigma that is India. This country has been dubbed the world's most multidimensional. Love it or loathe it, and most visitors see-saw between the two. India promises to jostle your entire being, and no matter where you go or what you do, it's a place you'll never forget."

After hearing Sai Baba's words, I flashed back a few years to November 2001, in New Jersey. A close friend and co-worker at the hospital had invited me to go with her to New Delhi, India, and stay with her family for the month of December. After reading heaps of information about India, I decided to ask my nursing supervisor for permission to take the month of December off and travel to New Delhi.

I was surprised by her ultimatum: "Diane I am very sorry but I can't grant you this request. You've taken so much time off with your travels already; it isn't fair to the rest of the nurses. December is the holiday season and others will want to take time off also. If you decide to go, you'll have to resign. You are a great asset to this hospital and I personally wouldn't want you to leave."

Oh wow! What was I to do? If I kept my job, I would forego a once-in-a-lifetime opportunity to stay with an Indian family and learn more about that country's remarkable and varied cultural teachings and traditions. If I quit my job and went to India, how would I pay the mortgage and all my other bills when I got back? After days of internal debate and knowing that traveling to India meant giving up a truly enjoyable and financially secure nursing job, I made the decision to fulfill my heart's desire! Yes, I would take my chances and trust that another nursing job would be available upon my return from India!

During that eventful December month, I experienced the magnificent Taj Mahal, which is a UNESCO world heritage site that symbolizes eternal love. I also traveled and explored on my own the vast religious temples, churches and mosques; including the Dalai Lama's Buddhist spiritual dwelling called Dharamsala in the upper ranges of the Northern Indian Kangra Valley. It was there that I became so severely sick that all I wanted to do was die. Barely managing to find enough strength to get out of bed at the small hotel where I was staying, I called my temporarily adopted Indian family who helped me arrange travel by private taxi back to their home in New Delhi—a 12-hour, very expensive car ride! What a monumental, frightening ordeal! Thankfully, with the help of healing herbs and loving care from my adopted Indian mom, the "nurse was nursed" back to health in about a week's time. To this day she remains one of my Earth angels.

My adopted mom buying herbs and vegetables outside their home.

Taj Mahal.

Once I got my strength back, about a week before returning home, I was alarmed to hear on the radio that terroristic threats were occurring in New Delhi and Mumbai, where political unrest and violence had been taking place. After the September 11th Twin Tower attacks in New York City that year, the Indian government was being very cautious and planning to delay air travel as a result of these threats. Hearing this news and beginning to feel desperate, I literally knelt down on my knees next to the bed and said, "God, please get me safely back home to New Jersey!"

A monkey meditating at Monkey Temple.

So, just three years later, it was no wonder I resisted the call to go back to India for a healing. I didn't want to go back to India! The poverty and poor living conditions were still extremely difficult for me to tolerate, and the memory of being so sick during my last visit still haunted me. Was I willing to risk getting so sick again and possibly dying?

After informing my sister about my impending return to India she said, "Diane you can't go to India. I just heard about all the alerts for travelers there."

I responded to her by saying, "I have decided to follow this vision because I believe it is part of God's plan for me. And if I need to risk my life to receive a healing there…so be it!"

With only two weeks to make plans and learn more about this mystical person named Sai Baba, I combed the Internet to learn of his whereabouts. I booked my flight, believing that he would be arriving at his Brindavan Ashram in Whitefield, outside of Bangalore, during the time he had instructed me to be in India. I was learning that Sai Baba is a spiritual educator and guru whose devotees purport him to be a miracle worker who has spent a lifetime serving humanity. On the International Sai Baba Organization website I read:

"I have come to light the lamp of Love in your hearts, to see that it shines day by day with added luster. I have not come on behalf of any exclusive religion. I have not come on a mission of publicity for a sect or creed or cause, nor have I come to collect followers for a doctrine. I have no plan to attract disciples or devotees into my fold or any fold. I have come to tell you of this unitary faith, this spiritual principle, this path of Love, this virtue of Love, this duty of Love, this obligation of Love." (4 July, 1968- Sai Baba)

Two weeks later, I landed in Bangalore, India, where I hired a taxi to take me to the ashram in Whitefield. Stepping out of the cab onto the street, I was shocked at what I saw. Extreme poverty abounding everywhere I looked! Small, smiling children—some of them missing an arm or leg—dressed in old, torn, dirty clothes, began to surround me and started begging. I was just as horrified as I was when I first visited India in 2001!

Walking through the gate into the ashram, and inquiring about nearby hotel accommodations for a week or so, a man told me, "Down the street is a nice hotel where many international travelers stay." He also said that I could obtain accommodations within the ashram, but that didn't appeal to me.

Dragging my heavy luggage down a dirty, garbage-littered street, lined with small shacks and tents selling all kinds of religious icons, jewelry and clothing, I finally reached the hotel with a great sigh of relief. After registering and walking up the two flights of stairs to my room, I plopped my exhausted body onto the bed.

Streets filled with piles of garbage.

Two hours later, I awoke and made the emotionally difficult walk back to the ashram. All I wanted to do was close my eyes and block out the sights of poverty and the endless number of beggars. I felt such pity for them! These negative thoughts and feelings were suddenly interrupted by the Voice within: "Open your eyes my child. Don't shine pity. Shine your Light. See them as whole, perfect beings. It doesn't serve to shed pity."

"Oh my God! I'm being shown and taught another powerful lesson right here and now," I thought. "Yes, it's true! People don't need pity." I slowly began to open my eyes, my heart and my arms to all who surrounded me. In that moment, I felt incredibly blessed with this wisdom.

Brindavan Ashram looked massive as I approached its gate and regarded the many buildings surrounding the complex. I learned from a devotee who had been waiting weeks to see him that Sai Baba had just arrived the day before. How very interesting! His timing coincided perfectly with what I heard in the vision. The devotee also informed me that *Darshan* takes place each morning and afternoon. *Darshan* is the Sanskrit Hindu word for receiving spiritual blessings from a guru.

Lining up along with many thousands of people outside the gate, I waited to be allowed to enter the massive Darshan Hall. Women sit on the floor on one side of the hall while men sit on the opposite side. The ushers packed us in like sardines. I started to feel the energy build as the time neared for Sai Baba to come out on stage. When he finally appeared, I was surprised to see how much he had aged compared to an image of him I had seen at a friend's house years ago. The massive crowd began chanting in Hindu, as Sai Baba prepared to speak. The love and devotion in the hall was indescribable. I sat quietly on the floor, waiting intently for this *healing* that I was supposed to receive. I never felt *anything*…not physically, anyway.

However, I did receive a healing after leaving the ashram. Despite being extremely conscious of what I was eating while exploring Kerala, southwest of Bangalore, I again developed a severe case of food poisoning. Having brought along sacred ash supposedly manifested by Sai Baba, I placed it on my belly and within a half hour, the symptoms miraculously disappeared.

Perhaps even more profoundly, I believe I was guided to go back to India to attain two very powerful lessons. First of all, I learned to not shine pity on the less fortunate ones, but instead to shine the Light of love from within my heart and see all as perfect.

The second lesson requires a little background knowledge. There were some serious allegations made against Sai Baba that generated media headlines around the world. I don't know if the allegations were true or false, but the multitudes of people who continue to revere Sai Baba show me he's making a spiritual difference for the masses on a huge scale. The empowering lesson learned here is, when I'm in my own truth, being of service with integrity… it doesn't matter what other people think about me!

Reflecting back on the original vision, I wonder if I actually heard Sai Baba's voice instructing me to go to India, or whether it was my intuition projecting Sai Baba's image telling me to go. It really doesn't matter. By choosing to return to India, I gained two invaluable life lessons, and I remain grateful for the guidance that led me there.

Chapter 13

"Go confidently in the direction of your dreams. Live the life you have imagined."
Henry David Thoreau

Emigrating to New Zealand

"Oh my! I really am relocating to a foreign country. Am I out of my mind?"

Sitting on my hammock out on the lanai, being gifted with a rainbow.

Over the years I've had many experiences listening to my intuition, but it has taken extreme amounts of practice to trust this inner Voice without judgment. I took a huge leap forward after my ayahuasca experience, so that now, when I get a thought or feeling, I intuitively act upon it. One day in June of 2005, while lying in the hammock on my lanai in Hawaii, my intuitive Voice told me to check out New Zealand's immigration site on the Internet. This thought seemed to fly into my consciousness out of nowhere.

Ever since visiting New Zealand in 2004, I had had a very strong feeling this country would eventually be my home for an extended period of time. Placing this *knowing* into the recesses of my subconscious, I allowed all to be revealed through Divine timing, so that by January of 2006, I was ready to make the huge transition from life in Hawaii to residing in New Zealand.

Emigrating to New Zealand sounds like a whole new world. Asking myself, "Do I have the courage to uproot my entire life and move to a foreign country?" I said with fortitude in my voice, "Yes! I will trust *intuitive knowing* and allow new chapters of my life to unfold."

Taking a deep breath, I began looking for answers by surfing the Internet and finding the New Zealand Immigration site, where I read: "If you are interested in migrating to New Zealand as a skilled migrant and if you have the skills we need, then you will need to fill out the *Expression of Interest* form." This form basically provides INZ (Immigration New Zealand) enough information to determine whether or not the applicant meets the initial requirements to become a citizen. Reviewing the long-term, skills-shortage list, I was pleasantly surprised to learn that Registered Nurses were needed; and I thought this may be my way to becoming an immigrant.

I also learned that I would have to meet the threshold of 100 points for what are called the "employability and capacity-building factors." According to INZ: "The points system is designed to reflect which applicants have the most to offer New Zealand so that INZ can extend invitations to apply for residence to them." Finally, after spending many long hours filling out the Expression of Interest form, I submitted the application, along with its steep monetary fee. The site also informed me that most people who apply for residency are not accepted because of the stringent application system. Even though this whole process was emotionally draining, I still felt I had an excellent chance of becoming a New Zealand resident. I just needed to keep trusting my Divine guidance.

A grueling six months of filling out forms followed, including providing the New Zealand nursing council detailed college transcripts and nursing employment history. Then I hired a nurse-recruiting agency from New Zealand to help me find a nursing job: a mandatory requirement before one can receive a Permanent Resident Visa. After a few telephone interviews, I was offered a job at a hospital on the North Island of New Zealand. Immediately I informed immigration that I had accepted a nursing position. A few weeks later I received a registered letter granting me the visa. Bingo! It's brilliant when a plan is manifested!

Let Love Lead the Way

Each and every time I trust my intuition, I realize I'm exactly where I need to be. Knowing the universe is supporting me every step of the way fuels my passion to continue along life's path.

"Oh my God! I really am relocating to a foreign country. Am I out of my mind?" I suddenly remembered an astrology reading I had a few years back. Informed by the astrologer that I would be living in a foreign country someday, my response at that time was, "Not I!"

After the shock waves of the imminent move wore off, I started reading about the North and South Islands of New Zealand and looked over the many photos taken during my last New Zealand visit in 2004.

One of many massive ancient trees in NZ.   *The family horse having lunch.*   *Sheep gathering together, eating the lush NZ green grass.*

I reflected on how naturally beautiful the country is, from the most peaceful virgin rainforests to the most powerful, untamed and pulse-pounding coastlines imaginable. New Zealand is pure and natural—a place where there are more sheep than people!

Once again, I tackled the tedious moving process of packing, selling furniture, and eliminating the *stuff* I didn't need any more. After hiring a moving company and saying goodbye to beloved friends, family, and Hawaii, I was ready to go, although I suspected some of my relatives thought I had lost my mind!

My next grand adventure awaited!

"Aloha Honu (turtle) and the Hawaiian Islands."

Chapter 14

"All that we need to know, all the wisdom of the cosmos, we will find in our hearts"
Mother Theresa

Message in the Cloud

"You are here to serve God. You will first need to die, but not physically." I turned my head to the left to see the Pyramid of the Sun. I then lifted my eyes up towards the clouds.

"Oh my God!"

Flying into Nelson, NZ.

Shortly after emigrating to New Zealand, on a weekend off from work, I decided to visit some special friends I had met on one of my Planet Earth adventures. I hopped on a plane for Nelson, a small city on the northern tip of the South Island, surrounded by the shores of the beautiful Tasman Bay, where tranquil seaside and bush land of native forest meet.

After graciously welcoming and embracing me with hugs at the airport, my friends showed me around this quaint small city. Nelson is a creative community filled with artists and craftspeople from all over the world. I loved the outside cafés, with their wide array of local gourmet food. Another scrumptious delight was the premium wines and the delicious goat's cheese. During one of our conversations, my friends asked, "Why don't you move here to Nelson, Diane?" For some strange reason, this thought kept buzzing around in my head throughout the weekend.

On Monday morning, before traveling back to the North Island, I decided to visit the personnel department at the local hospital in Nelson. To my amazement, the very same day, they offered me an easy nursing position that included a decent salary, no on-call nursing responsibilities and a great work schedule! In all my years of nursing, I have never had such a fantastic offer! To cut a long story short, I quit my nursing job in the North Island, moved to Nelson and accepted the Adolescent Nurse Coordinator's position at the hospital that March of 2006.

One day in late August, I received an email from a friend in Hawaii, asking if I would like to fly to Tonga to swim with the humpback whales. "Oh my God, would I ever!" With great anticipation, after receiving all the details, I registered with the facilitator, Celeste Eaton, for the two-week whale swim in October.

I had the distinct feeling I was again going to embark on some extended, new travel adventures, offering amazing discoveries and powerful learning experiences, which would require time off from work. So, my nursing career in New Zealand was short-lived.

A few days before leaving to swim with the humpback whales in Tonga, I was watching a TV show about Teotihuacan, the sacred site of the Aztec people, when, all of a sudden, my left toe started to ache. The pain intensified until I said aloud, "Okay, I will check out this place!" Remarkably, as soon as I said the words, the pain immediately stopped.

On October 3rd, I flew to Tonga and had two blissful weeks with Celeste, swimming with the "loving giants" of the sea. Celeste's website is www.celestialsonics.com

Swimming with humpback whales in Tonga.
If you look closely, you may see a heart on the upper left corner.

Leaving Tonga, photo taken in the window seat of the plane.

Then, in November 2006, after much contemplation, I flew from Nelson to Mexico to explore Teotihuacan. I had received numerous intuitive signs encouraging me to embrace the energies of this mysterious, prehistoric Aztec site. Teotihuacan was an ancient, religious capital and pilgrimage site for the Aztec people, dating back to 200 B.C. According to some, it was a ceremonial center for religious and civic expressions.

Surrounding the huge complex are three pyramids: the Pyramid of the Sun (the size of the Great pyramid of Giza), the Pyramid of the Moon, and the Pyramid of Quetzalcoatl, also known as the Feathered Serpent Pyramid.

Pyramid of the Moon.

Pyramid of the Sun

According to research done by Saburo Sugiyama at Arizona State University in 1966: "Teotihuacan arose as a new religious center in the Mexican Highlands around the time of Christ. Although its incipient period (the first two centuries B.C.) is poorly understood, archaeological data show that the next two centuries (Tzacualli to Miccaotli phases; A.D. 1-200) were characterized by monumental construction, during which Teotihuacan quickly became the largest and most populous urban center in the New World."

After traveling approximately 24 hours and crossing the International Date Line, I arrived in Mexico City. Going through immigration late at night is a nightmare. Exhausted and irritable from lack of sleep and having almost no patience left whatsoever, I cried out to my angels for help coping with the extremely long immigration line. I also asked for help finding the person who was to pick me up and take me to the hotel. After finally leaving immigration, while converting dollars to pesos at the ATM, I turned my head and, incredibly, saw a woman directly in front of me holding a sign with the name of my hotel for the night. I thanked my angels profusely!

The following day, November 11th, involved a bus ride to my next hotel in Teotihuacan. Fortunately, I had made these hotel reservations well in advance in order to be almost within walking distance of this remarkable, archeological site.

On the way to Teotihuacan, I enjoyed a leisurely tour of Mexico City, including a wonderful opportunity to visit the Shrine of Our Lady of Guadalupe, another aspect of the Virgin Mary.

At my hotel in Teotihuacan I was pleased to discover a taxi that routinely, throughout the day, shuttled people to the famous site and back for only $2 a day. What a deal! I unpacked and scheduled the taxi for Teotihuacan within the hour. I didn't want to miss the chance to put my feet on this sacred site on this particularly auspicious day, 11-11.

Entering Teotihuacan for the first time, I immediately became aware of an energy that was so powerful I almost lost my balance. I promptly closed my eyes in reverence and said a blessing of grace. Looking around this huge complex, I felt like a "kid in a candy store," wanting to explore the entire site in one afternoon. Knowing this was impossible, I reminded myself to slow down, take a deep breath and allow the energy to flow throughout my body.

Before I knew it, a guard was telling me the site was closing and I would have to leave. Fortunately, a taxi driver was there to drive me back to the hotel.

The next morning I awoke with a pounding headache, feeling like an 18-wheeler truck had run over my body and not just once! "I wonder where I went while sleeping last night?" I asked myself before taking a relaxing, warm shower. My headache soon subsided and I returned to Teotihuacan to climb the Pyramids of the Sun and Moon. By early afternoon I began to feel extremely tired. All I wanted to do was go back to the hotel and rest. But I couldn't leave until I had climbed the third pyramid and said a blessing of gratitude to my guardian angels for getting me to Mexico and for guiding me safely to this magnificent, healing place.

Despite my fatigue, I slowly climbed the Pyramid of the Feathered Serpent. Reaching the top, as I bowed and offered a prayer of gratitude, I heard from within a powerful, firm voice:

Entrance steps of Pyramid of Feathered Serpent

"You are here to serve God. You will first need to die, but not physically." I intuitively turned my head to the left to see the Pyramid of the Sun. I lifted my eyes up towards the clouds.

"Oh my God!" I can't believe what I am seeing. Camera in hand, I took several photographs.

Image in the cloud, Teotihuacan.

"Message in the Cloud"
Close-up image as shown on front cover.

Before I describe what I saw, I suggest that you gaze at the image and allow the energy of the photo to speak to you instead. My intention is only to present this material and you, the reader, can decide if you resonate with it.

Seeing what appears to be a man's face, I question this presence inwardly. "Who are you?" I hear one word reply,

"Christ."

"WOW! Have I just photographed Christ?"

I couldn't wait to get back to the hotel. I wanted to ask some of the staff who they believe the face in the photo looks like. Back then, I still had some doubts about what I was regularly seeing or hearing and wasn't sure if it was my ego or my guardian angel expressing itself.

I walked into the hotel restaurant and sat down, completely exhausted, bursting with anticipation. A waiter approached and asked what I would like to order. Before he finished telling me the "specials" of the day, I pulled out my camera and showed him the photograph. I asked in an inquiring tone, "Who do you think that face looks like?" He answered assuredly,

"Oh! That is Dios Jesucristo." The waiter then called over other waiters and they all agreed the face is Christ revealing himself in the cloud. We were completely in awe!

I also see another face to the left of Christ, a child whispering into His ear.

When I look closely in-between them, I can see a whale tail. When I look to the right of the Christ's head, I see a butterfly.

The images and message that I have been receiving in the cloud are quite profound. As I continue on my path of self-discovery and transformation, the messages become ever more clear. I am here on this planet to serve by learning how to "shine my Light" unconditionally.

Chapter 15

"When I speak my truth, I honor and love myself."
Heart Moon

The Mystifying Face in Peru

I was astounded to see a face in a cloud appearing very similar to, perhaps exactly like the one I experienced in Teotihuacan. "Am I truly being spiritually watched over and taken care of?"

While surfing the Internet and still living in New Zealand, I stumbled upon an adventure that sounded extraordinary: a guided trip to Peru. I became quite fascinated thinking about exploring the amazing Amazon Rainforest and sacred Inca sites, including Machu Picchu. Also included in this impressive journey was the intriguing option of partaking in some of Mother Earth's master plant medicines. After reviewing the itinerary, I felt in my gut that this was another "life chapter" that I didn't want to miss. I *knew* it would push me past my comfort level and teach me priceless lessons, so I decided to register.

Shortly after making this decision in late January 2008, I felt the call to leave New Zealand and return to the Hawaiian Islands; so I packed up all my belongings and said goodbye to my friends. First I successfully applied for an indefinite New Zealand Permanent Residency Visa, which allows me to return to New Zealand and stay as long as I like. I am thinking that perhaps this is why I felt a strong pull to emigrate to New Zealand in the first place. Someday, I may wish to return and live there again. I'm very fortunate to have manifested this visa. Most applicants are denied permanent residency and are often refused, despite having legal representation and engaging in many years of negotiations.

A short while after resettling in Honolulu, I flew to Lima, Peru, to meet up with my 13 journey mates. Flying to Lima is, in itself, an adventure of trust. With two stopovers in Canada—one in Vancouver and the other in Toronto—I was thinking, "I have less than an hour to get off this plane in Vancouver, pick up my luggage, go through customs and go to another gate to board the connecting flight to Toronto!"

Unable to stop thinking about this and with some anxiety in my voice, I asked the flight attendant, "Will I have enough time to make the connecting flight?"

"Yes, you'll be just fine," she assured me.

After landing in Vancouver, the worries resurfaced when I was unable to spot my bags in the baggage claim area, especially after everyone else had already collected their luggage and gone off to customs! "Of all the times to lose my luggage this has got to be the worst!" I told myself. Blood pressure rising by the second, taking a deep breath, I said to myself, "Let it go! I will somehow deal with it."

I surrendered to the fact that I may miss out on this grand adventure if I miss my connecting flights or if I arrive there without my luggage. I would most likely not be able to fly with the group to Iquitos, where we are scheduled to meet our trip facilitator to begin our journey.

Then, all of a sudden, out of *nowhere*, I spotted my luggage! I literally did a double take. It just appeared! Not lingering to question my eyesight, I picked up my luggage, quickly passed through customs and ran as fast as I could, hearing my luggage bouncing behind me. I managed to get to the gate with just a few minutes to spare.

"Wow, I am so grateful to be boarding this plane," I said to the flight attendant. I relaxed with the knowledge that all is well, however I began to suspect the journey to Peru was going to be an adventure filled with challenges, excitement, and lessons of spiritual surrender.

After long flights to Lima, where I connected with other group members, and to Iquitos to meet the facilitator, we spent a couple of days of sightseeing around Iquitos. Then we boarded an ancient, rundown ferry on a late afternoon for the 14-hour ride down the Amazon River to the jungle camp where we were to stay for a week. On the somewhat shoddy top deck that is reserved for first class passengers, our facilitator reminded us that Peru is a "Third World Country" and first class accommodations are not quite up to the standards to which most Westerners are accustomed. I was reminded how blessed I am to experience personal abundance on a regular basis.

I also realized that exploring the Amazon Rainforest presents challenges—such as lots and lots of mosquitoes! Not being a fan of DEET, I use instead essential oils of lavender, eucalyptus, neem seed oil, B-complex supplement and organic oregano oil, all of which help to heal or prevent itchy bug bites. I've been told that adding a few drops of organic oregano oil to the water or under your tongue also helps to kill the nasty bacteria and viruses that thrive in the Amazon Rainforest.

During the ferry ride I agreed to partake in a sacred plant medicine that I was offered, hoping to receive clarity about this adventure. Although generally not a fan of ingesting drugs of any sort, when it comes to taking master plant medicines from the Amazon Rainforest, I humbly trusted them to bring more understanding into my life.

Sunset on the Amazon River.

Before ingesting, I said a blessing and imagined a vision of delight and bliss. Listening to the majestic Amazon birds singing love songs during an exquisite sunset, I thought to myself, "What a wondrous place this is for a mini-vision quest! Mother Nature's magnificence is truly on display!"

An hour or so after taking the plant medicine, I drifted off for an extended time into deep meditation. In this relaxed state, I began having a vision and received a clear message that at first distressed me. I was being shown that all desires and material goals are unimportant and for the first time in my life I didn't care what people were thinking about me. I also found myself receiving this vision with total detachment.

Afterwards I opened my eyes, easily bringing myself back to conscious awareness. Utterly confused, I asked my guardian angels, "How can this be? Why am I on this planet if it doesn't matter whether or not I manifest my desires and goals?"

I decided to ask one of the group members what all this meant. Her response was simple and direct. "How wonderful to be experiencing this! Detachment is a great lesson."

Contemplating what she said for a very long while, I reached the realization that, by not clinging tightly to people, places, and things, I am able to achieve the freedom I'm looking for. There is nothing to fear when there is nothing to lose! I also began to understand the importance of speaking my truth. Whenever I speak my truth, I honor and love myself. And when I truly love myself, I'm able to personally experience God as unconditional "Love and Light."

Later on during this adventurous Amazon River journey, I was astonished to see a face in a cloud that looks very similar to, perhaps even exactly the same, as the cloud face I saw in Teotihuacan. This experience prompted the internal question: "Am I truly being watched over and taken care of? And to be able to photograph this "being"— how astounding is that?"

In the center of the cloud is the familiar face.

Close-up view.

As we near the jungle camp, even though I've had very little sleep, I realized the boat ride itself had provided me with a truly inspirational learning experience. After disembarking the ferry around 5 a.m., our group walked to a small village called Genaro Herrera. After eating breakfast and sleeping in hammocks for a few hours, we climbed into dugout canoes and traveled a few hours more in pouring rain before arriving at our new home deep in the Amazon jungle. Soaked from head to toe, I stepped out of the canoe reminding myself, "At least I'm warm and somehow I'm going to have fun!"

One of the many challenges I faced there in the jungle was overcoming my fear of bathing with *fish that bite* in the cold and murky Amazon tributary waters. I also tried not to focus on possibly encountering pit vipers lurking around in the river and searching for something like "me" to sink their poisonous fangs into!

However, after two days of not bathing and starting to smell a little funky, I finally got up the nerve to cautiously place one foot in front of the other and enter the muddy water. I achieved a personal record by managing to take a bath and wash my hair in less than a minute! Having great respect for Mother Nature, I used the organic, environmentally friendly products our facilitator suggested we bring.

Our camp and the tributary where I bathed and later fell in the mud.

Stepping out of the water, I realized the bathing experience wasn't nearly as terrible as I thought it would be. But then again… most things I fear turn out better than I imagine.

All of the staff that our fearless leader had hired—native Peruvians skilled in jungle navigation and survival—were exceptionally helpful and patient with us. Two nights in a row, during their nightly rounds, they found pit vipers crawling around in the rafters of our huts. The pit viper is one of the most poisonous jungle snakes; being bitten by one generally means death, especially in places where there are no hospitals or ambulances! Fortunately the snakes were caught without any of us getting hurt or bitten. Unfortunately, they are thrown into the fire and burned to death, which is a terrible thing to witness.

While in the jungle, we had the option to partake in three ayahuasca ceremonies. I chose not to participate because I didn't feel the need at that time to ingest the ayahuasca to connect with the plant's healing energy. I still have flashbacks of this experience in my life and over the years I have gained a deep respect for this plant.

After five long days in the jungle, we said our goodbyes to those who helped us, including the shaman (curandero) and the local villagers.

Approaching the dugout canoe, carrying all my belongings, I slipped and fell, beginning another challenge. My clean, dry clothes, my luggage and I were covered with wet, very thick mud! Being *so* pissed off, I slowly got up with a huge attitude problem. I realized right away it was better to let go of these negative feelings and surrender to what was. It was not an easy task, but I knew if I didn't, the canoe ride back to the village of Genero Herrera would be miserable and I would miss out experiencing the pure, raw beauty of the Amazon jungle. Making the wise choice to surrender, I settled down and appreciated the splendor of the journey.

The curious seekers.

Arriving in Genero Herrera, we boarded the ferry back to Iquitos. Despite the physical and mental difficulties including living in the Amazon jungle without Western comforts, getting to know the local tribal families and traditions was truly an incredible and powerful learning experience.

Once back in Iquitos I felt so blessed to be staying at a five-star hotel where hot showers and a clean, comfortable bed without mosquitoes buzzing in my ears was *so* wonderful! That luxury felt like I had died and gone to Heaven! I went to sleep that night feeling tremendous gratitude for the simple comforts I sometimes take for granted.

After staying and refreshing ourselves in Iquitos for another few days, we departed for Cuzco and Machu Picchu.

Chapter 16

"I can see, and that is why I can be happy, in what you call the dark, but which to me is golden. I can see a God-made world, not a manmade world."
Helen Keller

The Spirit of the Fire

The pain intensified to the point where I had to do something. Just what to do, I didn't know at first.

Flying over the Andes Mountains to Cuzco and seeing the peaks jutting proudly upwards toward the Heavens is a spectacular, unforgettable sight. Sitting peacefully in the window seat, I wondered what lessons the second half of this journey would reveal.

Plaza de Cuzco

After arriving in Cuzco, I became acutely aware of the altitude change to approximately 9,000 feet above sea level. We were offered coca leaf to drink and chew, because the native South American plant is often used to help acclimate to high altitude. We were advised to take it easy and go slowly while venturing out and exploring, especially on our first day.

The following morning I woke up to a pounding headache; most likely due to the altitude. After taking a couple of ibuprofen and drinking some coca tea, a few hours later I felt like a new person, ready to venture out and explore Cuzco.

Thank goodness I had purchased a handmade, thick wool sweater in Lima before flying to the much-colder Cuzco. Walking into a Catholic Church and seeing a statue of Mother Mary, I offered prayers of peace and took a photo of her. To my surprise I saw a PEP in my viewfinder. Remembering to take another photo immediately, I saw that it had disappeared, which is typical PEP behavior.

PEP on the lower right side of the framed picture in a Catholic Church in Cuzco.

I took another photo immediately after. The PEP has disappeared.

Over the next couple of days, we traveled via bus to the Sacred Valley of the Incas, where we explored and climbed the Inca ruins, including Ollayantambo. We also had a chance to shop in the small village of Pisac with its market filled with an abundant assortment of locally-made Indian crafts and colorful clothing.

Having an intimate moment with the locals.

In Ollayantambo, we had the opportunity to experience "San Pedro," another master plant medicine. Our ceremonial guide, Victor, is a San Pedro Curandero (traditional healer) raised in the Peruvian shamanic tradition. I was quite apprehensive about taking San Pedro for the first time, as it meant stepping into the unknown again!

Victor's explanations about what San Pedro is and what we possibly may experience reassured me about drinking it. San Pedro is very sacred and an integral part of Andean and Coastal shamanism. I also liked Victor's message. He spoke from his heart and emphasized the importance of healing ourselves, which will ultimately have a positive impact on healing Mother Earth.

We can choose how many cups of San Pedro to drink, though the maximum is seven. We drank our first cup in the early evening session at the hotel, after performing a ceremony honoring the plant, and an hour later we traveled by van to a secluded, sacred Inca spot not far from the hotel.

The night air was very cold and I sensed a tinge of frost starting to form on the bushes. The stars shone brilliantly in the cloudless sky as we sat on the ground watching one of Victor's helpers build a roaring fire. Victor then offered us a second cup of San Pedro. Because my body is very sensitive, I declined the offer. I wanted to experience the effects of the first cup before ingesting more.

Lying down in the fetal position on the cold, hard earth next to the fire, I slowly began feeling a physical pain in my heart, radiating down to my solar plexus. The pain intensified to the point where I had to do something. Just what to do, I didn't know at first.

All of a sudden, I realized I had to give the pain to the fire. As I started to release years and years of emotional pain from my heart chakra, I immediately felt relief. I was in total amazement for two reasons. I realized I still had a lot of blocked heart pain, and secondly, the spirit of the fire was actually relieving my pain. Fire for me symbolizes Light and I believe we are all made of Light. In the Bible, Yahweh (the one true God) manifested Himself in various forms of fire on many different occasions. Examples include: the making of the Covenant with Abraham (Gen. 15:17), the burning bush (Exo. 3:2-4), the pillar of fire (Exo. 13:21), on Sinai (Exo. 19:18), in the flame on the altar (Judg. 13:20), and Yahweh answered by fire (1 Kings 18:24, 38).

Throughout the night, I continued releasing waves of emotional pain that no longer served me. At one point, glancing up at the sky, seeing millions of stars twinkling brightly with "Mama Moon" watching faithfully over me, I sent prayers of gratitude to the San Pedro plant and for the healing I was receiving. I also had a strong sense that Victor was actively participating in our healing.

After the ceremony ended at 3:30 a.m., we gave thanks to Victor, his helpers, and all the spirits who assisted in this amazing journey, after which we went back to the hotel to complete the San Pedro experience on our own.

The next day, we took the train from Ollantaytambo to Aquas Calientes, a village at the foot of Machu Picchu. The two-hour journey wound through the stunning Urubamba River Valley, with its scenic views of picturesque, glacier mountain peaks.

We arrived mid-morning in Aquas Calientes, a bustling village filled with tourists from all over the world. I wondered where Machu Picchu was and was told this "Lost City of the Incas" sits high in the Peruvian cloud forest, invisible from the town below.

In the early afternoon, we met our guide, who was steeped in Andean shamanism. He would lead us to Machu Picchu and interpret the various sections of the Lost City and what they were used for. With much anticipation, we boarded one of the many buses that transport people to the base of Machu Picchu.

*The magical spot at Machu Picchu.
Wayna Picchu is the huge mountain behind Machu Picchu.*

After passing through the admissions gate, we were instructed to hold hands and close our eyes as our guide led us to a magical spot.

Unable to contain my enthusiasm, I opened my eyes just before we were told to. Wow, what a spectacular view of Machu Picchu! It is one of the most magnificent sights I've ever seen! Over the many years of wanting to come here, I've seen many photos, but being here physically is a totally different experience. The energy radiating from this Lost City of the Incas is literally overpowering. I understand now why Machu Picchu is recognized as one of the most spiritual places on this planet!

During the afternoon, we all participate in a ceremony honoring this magical place. Our guide suggested we set intentions for both the planet and ourselves, to allow and trust that these intentions be manifested. After digging a small hole next to a pine tree, I placed my intentions inside and included a coin I had brought from New Zealand. I wasn't sure why, but, since I first found out about this trip while living in New Zealand, I thought that perhaps there's some connection between the Lost City of the Incas and New Zealand.

A PEP in the forest at Machu Picchu.

Entrance path at Wayna Picchu

We spent the rest of the afternoon exploring the sacred Temple of the Condor and the Temple of the Sun. According to some, Machu Picchu played a key role politically, socially, and religiously in the Incan Empire.

The next day I awoke at 4 a.m. and walked to the bus station, where I waited in a long line for a ride to the base of Machu Picchu. The rest of the group had decided to sleep in, but I wanted to climb Wayna Picchu, the mountain located at the back end of Machu Picchu and rising to 8,920 feet above sea level. According to the local guides, Wayna Picchu (in Quechua, the Native American language of South America) means "Young Peak." In the past, high priests who lived at the top of the summit, along with local virgins, greeted each morning with prayers and blessings.

We were advised to walk from the base of Machu Picchu to the Wayna Picchu gate entrance at least an hour before it opens. A total of only 400 visitors are allowed per day.

When the gate finally opened at 7 a.m. there were hundreds of people in line behind me. Before climbing we were required to sign an entrance permit and waiver. The need for this would soon become evident.

Full of energy and excitement, I started the climb. The trail quickly became very narrow and slippery with very steep steps.

Thank goodness there were steel cables at the narrowest sections to support my climb. According to the brochures, the climb to the summit should only take one hour, but it's been over an hour and I'm only half way up the mountain. I convinced myself that I was taking my time to enjoy the incredibly beautiful cloud formations and an amazing sunrise over the mountain ranges.

Reaching the summit and feeling elated as well as exhausted, I nevertheless decided to climb half way back down and take another path leading to the back of Wayna Picchu in order to visit the Temple of the Moon. It would be another hour or two before I reached this destination. During the climb down, I soon discovered that my stamina was short lived and my legs were beginning to shake. Thinking, "I don't think I can make it. I am so tired!" I then intuitively heard, "Yes you can!" I continued very slowly to walk for another 15 minutes up and down the steep, thick jungle trail.

Soon I said out loud, "I can't make it!" And once more I heard intuitively, "Yes you can." I stopped dead in my tracks, with tears running down my face, yelling out loud to the Voice I was hearing, "I need help!" Miraculously, I immediately felt a surge of energy. Once again I was able to start walking, and within 20 minutes I saw the Temple of the Moon. "What a relief!"

After taking some photos and feeling totally depleted, I lay down on the grass and fell asleep. A short time later, I awoke feeling much more rested and completely content. I got up, saying a prayer for peace for humanity, and began the descent back to the entrance of Wayna Picchu.

I felt such a sense of accomplishment. Hurray! My intuition was correct. I could make it up and behind Wayna Picchu, even when I didn't think it was possible. Again, I realized the importance of always trusting my intuition.

I met the rest of my group walking to the bus stop, and together we returned to Lima for our flights back home. I felt truly blessed for the many amazing insights I gained throughout my travels in Peru and thankful for being willing and able to trust and venture *into the unknown*.

Diane feeling elated reaching the summit of Wayna Picchu.

Chapter 17

"Somewhere, something incredible is waiting to be known."
Carl Sagan

The Cross of Light Phenomena

For the next two and half hours, standing in her unlit bathroom, inches from the window, we were mesmerized by this extraordinary phenomenon.

Sometimes an extraordinary phenomenon does occur in our ordinary, everyday life. By following my intuition I was led to discover what has been called the "Cross of Light." This incredible adventure started back in 2007, when I decided to travel about and enjoy the raw beauty of New Zealand, where I lived at that time. For over a month, I explored the South Island and afterwards, ferried my car over to the North Island, where this amazing story began.

Driving along the East Coast, I saw a sign indicating a retreat center up ahead. Saying out loud to myself, "I need to check this place out!" I immediately began to feel a tingling sensation running throughout my body as I drove up the bumpy, dirt driveway. A builder working on the property informed me that the retreat owner was not home. Feeling quite disappointed, I left my business card and continued on to find a place to stay the night.

Around 6 p.m., after settling in at an oceanfront campsite, I received a call on my cell phone from Elizabeth, the owner of the retreat. I told her a little about my spiritual journey and how I was drawn to check out her place. To my surprise she said, "I think you were drawn to come to my place so I could take you to meet my friend." Initially I declined, feeling very tired from the day's drive, but Elizabeth's persistence persuaded me to drive back to her house, where we then would go to meet this mysterious woman.

While changing my clothes, I heard the familiar, faint inner Voice telling me to bring my laptop. I grabbed it and drove to the retreat center, where I found Elizabeth waiting for me at her doorstep with a cheerful smile. Jumping into her car, we took off to visit the "mystery woman."

Entering her friend's home, Elizabeth introduced me to the lady we will call "Violet." I instantly felt a deep connection with her and we bonded quickly. The evening continued with sharing and talking until the wee hours of the night. At one point I opened my laptop and showed them my photos of the PEP taken at sacred sites from around the world. They were fascinated and I knew that someday Violet and I would meet again.

That "again" occurred in December 2009, after I had gone back to live in Hawaii. That summer, I once more felt the strong desire to revisit New Zealand, and I flew back in September. Towards the end of a four-month stay, I called Violet, who urged me to come and see her, explaining that she had something extraordinary to show me. Depending at that time upon public transportation, I took a very long 12-hour bus ride to Violet's place. We rejoiced at seeing each other again.

Over lunch, Violet told me how a light phenomenon began occurring in her bathroom window in 2008 and had continued to appear every night, becoming most brilliant as the night sky darkens. Furthermore, she had found several sites on the Internet talking about this exact manifestation, which has been termed the Cross of Light. I learned that the Cross of Light appeared in 1988 in California. On May 27 that year, the *Pasadena Star News* wrote: "Residents reported seeing a cross shining through a bathroom window of an apartment in El Monte." An eyewitness, Mona LaVine stated that she saw, "a cross of a pale golden Light…and simply beautiful." Margaret

Romero, owner of the place, had the glass replaced, but the Cross kept shining. According to the Internet and newspaper articles, the Cross of Light has revealed itself in countries around the world.

Sitting outside after dinner, Violet and I gazed at the neighbors' cows nonchalantly roaming the pasture in the warm, summer evening. As the clear night sky began to darken, Violet called me into her bathroom to see the Cross of Light, which was beginning to form on the window. For the next two and half hours, standing in her unlit bathroom, inches from the window, we were mesmerized by this extraordinary phenomenon. As the night progressed, the Cross just became brighter and brighter and more defined. I then noticed two similar crosses shining on either side of the first one! They were much bigger and appeared to be shining from outside. Walking outside to investigate, I saw the night was very dark, and surprisingly, there was no evidence of light, neither in the window nor in the yard!

Cross starting to form; palm tree outside of the window still visible. (New Zealand)

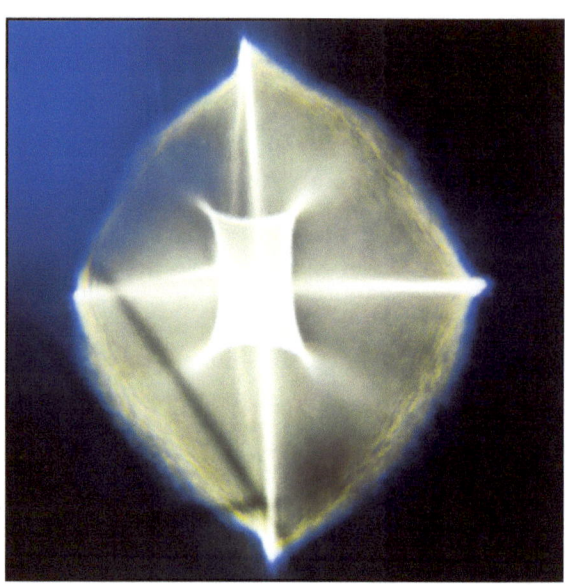

Fully formed Cross of Light. (New Zealand)

Looking at the Cross of Light intently, we both felt drawn to its center, where we had the clear sense of a doorway or passageway existing. As my heart started pounding, I reached out and held Violet's hand. We looked into one another's eyes and then back to the cross. "WOW!" We stayed bathed in this energy for hours. Using my Canon 5D SLR camera, I took numerous pictures without the flash.

To my astonishment, around 10:30 p.m., the cross simply vanished but reappeared for Violet at 5 a.m. the following day. According to her, this is not unusual. Later that evening, the cross reappeared around 8 p.m. and remained until late that night.

"This is truly an amazing anomaly that is occurring in your house," I said to Violet before saying farewell and leaving to prepare for my flight back to Hawaii.

On May 6, 2010, I received an email from Violet saying, "I am including the golden Cross of Light photo taken with my little cell phone. This was really taken in the daylight. There were no lights on anywhere. Some rare times the Cross of Light appears like fire."

Gazing at this "Golden Cross," I reflected back to an earlier time when I was meditating on my bed one evening in New Jersey. During the meditation, I asked my angels to join me. I then imagined myself being

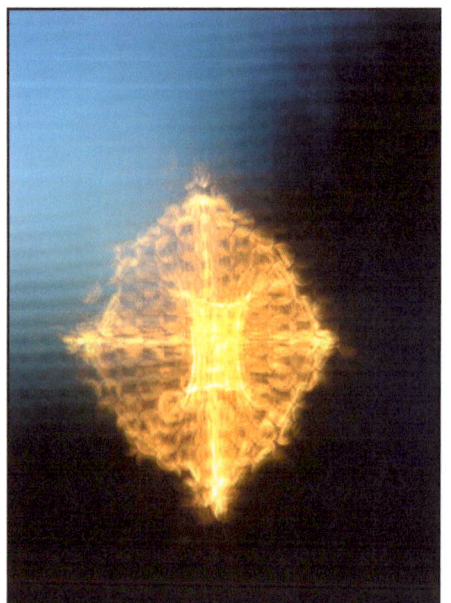

"Golden Cross of Light", NZ

bathed in a beautiful bubble of white Light. I then heard in my mind, as clear as day, "Not white Light but golden Light." I didn't understand the significance of this message until now.

In Mid-August of 2010, my friends Edith and Joseph attended one of my workshop presentations on the Big Island. They were fascinated to see photographs of the Cross of Light, and to learn that the Cross with its four-cornered portal, or doorway, has been showing up inexplicably in residential windows in both New Zealand and California.

Later that month, Edith and Joseph were visiting Carlsbad, California, doing repairs at their vacation rental home and visiting family. The second day after their arrival, they were astounded to discover a bright, vivid, silvery-white Cross of Light radiating through their guest bathroom window in the evening. They took pictures and forwarded them to me. I decided to fly to Carlsbad to experience and photograph the phenomena personally.

After my arrival in September, I discerned that Crosses of Light were visible in several different locations; in both gold and silvery white formations, depending on which direction one looked through the window. Somewhat skeptical at first, Joseph thought the crosses were being created by some kind of amazing light refraction caused by street light coming through the frosted glass window. However, I discovered the next day in the later afternoon that the Cross of Light became plainly visible even in broad daylight. Being so bright in daylight, it was a little difficult to photograph.

The four-cornered portals within each of the crosses appear very similar to those found within all other reported Cross-of-Light sightings. As of this writing, the Carlsbad crosses seem to be the first new apparitions of 2010 reported by anyone, anywhere so far.

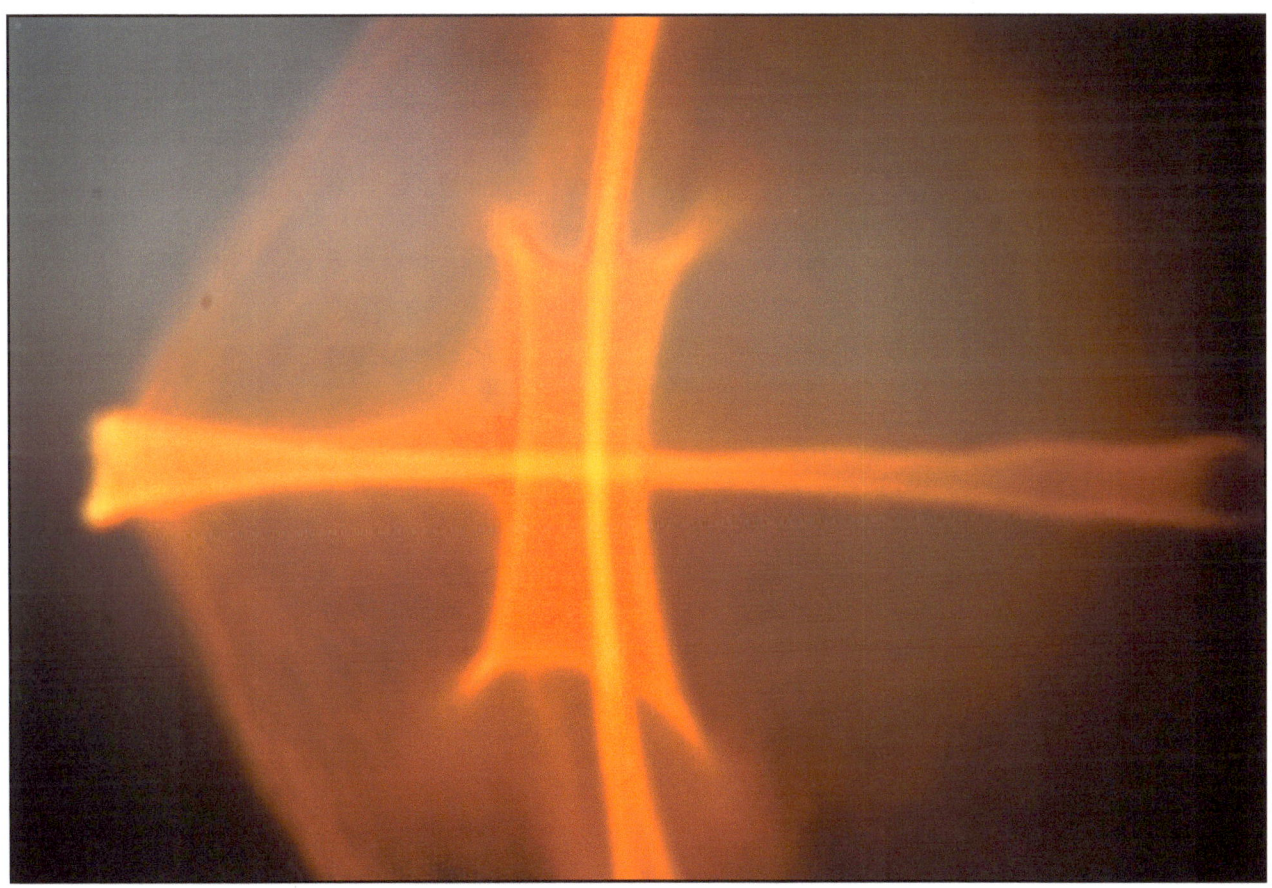

Night shot of Cross of Light in California.

 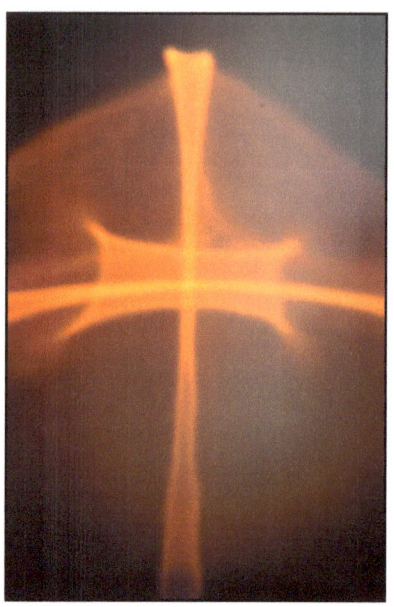

The silvery Cross of Light taken at night in NZ 2009, as shown on the back cover.

Cross of Light in CA 2010 rotated 90 degrees.

The Cross of Light is being viewed and utilized in many different ways. Some use it as a focus for meditation, some place the image next to themselves while they pray and some place images of the crosses throughout their homes. The messages that people report are always filled with love and healing. For some, it is a specific answer to a question, for others, it is a revelation. Such was the case for Cathy, a 51-year-old woman who placed it next to her bed and woke up realizing that a void she had been trying to fill for a lifetime had now been filled. Where she had previously been experiencing an ongoing sense of loneliness, she now felt a great peace and deep love had taken its place.

Personally, the Cross of Light has given me the assurance that I am cared for at all times. Now feeling guided and free of most fears, I feel a deeper connection to God, and have learned to trust my intuition more than ever. Violet, on the other hand, received a simple, yet profound, message to "be still," a message which has greatly enhanced her spiritual journey.

I believe that everyone using the cross receives exactly what he or she personally needs. For me, the Cross of Light represents a universal symbol for Love. I previously had an experience in 2005 while meditating, when I was guided through a doorway similar to the cross's portal, where I experienced my Divine Self as a Being of Light. Despite my resistance and fear of the unknown, I was ultimately able to trust my guardian angel and travel through that doorway. The transformation that I experienced back then gave me the faith and courage to follow my intuition or Divine guidance, which led me to discover Violet and the Cross of Light.

In today's chaotic world, many people are experiencing uncertainty, subsequently battling stress, anxiety and loneliness. I encourage people to trust and enter the "doorway" of the Cross of Light and surrender to potential transformation. In my experience, transformation can be quite subtle and may not seem to relate to everyday life. Often one simply starts to feel stronger and healthier, or just begins experiencing more enjoyment, contentment and peace of mind.

(Please note: the names of many people mentioned in this chapter have been changed to protect their privacy).

The following are some of the numerous testimonials I received after presenting the Cross of Light at my workshops.

"In the summer of 2003, I was living on the Mendocino coast of Northern California, Little River to be exact. I meditated weekly with a dedicated group of kindred spirits in Elk by the Sea. They had heard of the Cross of Light, being a phenomena [sic] happening in the world. This was the first that I had heard of it. Weeks later, as I entered my small bathroom, there shining in the window was the Cross. I not only quickly checked to see if there was any explanation for it outside (a light source), which there wasn't, but also retrieved my camera, to take pictures. It continued to stay for several hours, long enough for several friends to witness this miracle. I felt as if I was anointed by angelic Light that night, validating the spiritual path I am following to this day." DeBorah Jones

"After Heart Moon handed me the 5x7 picture of the Cross of Light, I was overjoyed that she gifted me such a beautiful picture and rare phenomena but that was nothing in comparison to the feeling I felt a few minutes later. I was walking back to my room and sort of star gazing and glancing down at the picture when I got in my room and stopped walking. I just stared at it and slowly rotated it clockwise. I reached a point/position where I just stopped spinning it and all of a sudden I felt waves upon waves of energy, starting from my head and going all the way down to my toes, goose bumps; and at the same time my eyes just began to fill with tears. I wasn't afraid—I didn't know what was going on though. I was just hit with this very powerful, very good feeling, and the tears were from joy, it felt like. It was a happy feeling for sure, I just was saying in my head "What the heck is going on here? This picture is talking to me or something." This continued for, oh I'd say a few minutes, five tops, gradually reducing in intensity until my skin was smooth and eyes were dry. I thank you Heart Moon for sharing such an amazing beautiful thing with me." With love, Adam.

"Heart Moon gave me a wonderful tool to help create a sacred space for myself and others before sharing my music. Her Cross of Light photograph and presentation was truly a life changing, powerful experience." EL

"I was able to revisit my child-like wonder and simplicity by focusing on the Cross of Light photo. It was an amazingly, insightful experience. Heart Moon's presentation was an in-depth voyage within." ML

"I very much enjoyed your workshop and hearing the others' experiences. For me, I felt a strong connection with my heart, the screen gently moving in the breeze synchronizing with my heartbeat. I felt heat around my heart and I also felt a lot of joy. Thank you for an inspiring afternoon. Love and best wishes." Sonia xx

"When I tune into receiving from this picture I can only describe what I felt as being a high frequency of clarity and love; purity is also a word that can attempt to describe this indescribable phenomena!" JA

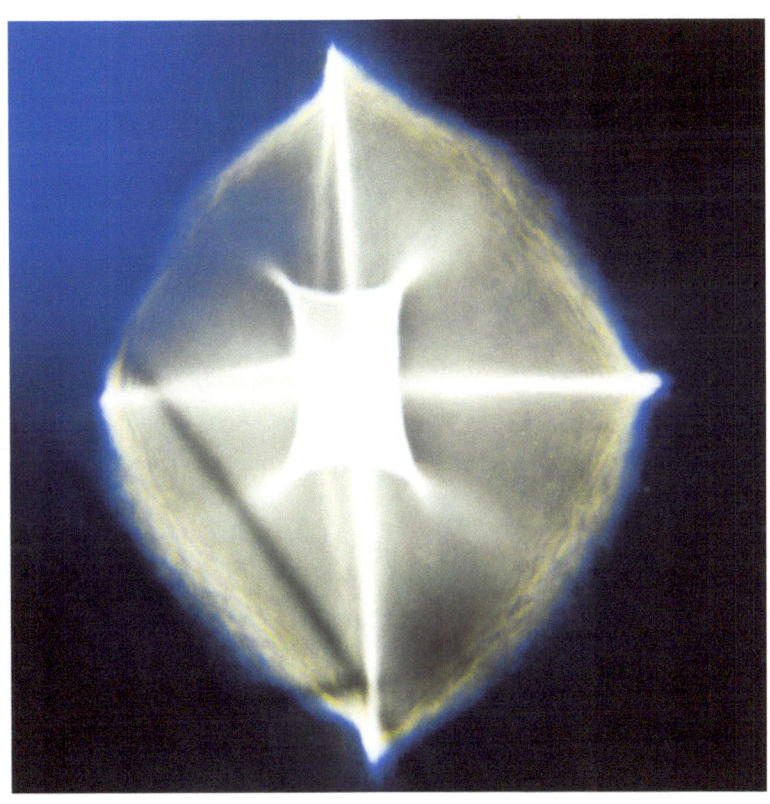

Epilogue

> "I have no idea where I am going on this path I call life.
> I continue to trust in my intuition and do my best to be
> kind to all living beings, knowing I will arrive home safely."
> Heart Moon

The Heart of the Moon, Again!

I whispered to Mama Moon, "I love you so much! Thank you for all your help."

Sitting at my desk writing *Intuitive Adventures beyond the Camera Lens,* I looked at my calendar and saw that it was already July 17, 2010. I was momentarily interrupted with a thought buzzing around in my head: "Now is the time to create my new website before my book gets published." After thinking of heaps of names, photographicenergyphenomena.com feels fitting for the messages I am conveying to my readers. The new website was launched on my birthday, September 2, 2010. In April 2011, the website was transformed along with a new name called heartmoonphotography.com

On September 24, 2010, during the full moon, I awoke suddenly at 4:30 in the morning. I quietly walked out onto the lanai where I was living and noticed the moon shining radiantly in the dark, cloudless sky. After getting my 5D camera from my bedroom, I gazed at the moon for the longest time before clicking away with my camera.

Excited, and wanting to see the photos I had taken, I downloaded them to my computer later that morning.

The 2010 full moon

My eyes were drawn to one of the photos I took. Zooming in, I was astonished to see once again, for only the second time, that the full moon had been transformed into a heart shape on its own.

When I introduce myself, more often than not, I usually say, "Hi, my name is Heart Moon." I decided to call myself Heart Moon after photographing the full moon in 2001, when it had transformed into a heart shape after developing the film. The name means so much to me because, as I have said earlier in this book, I truly believe my mom was instrumental in making this happen. How? I don't have a clue! More often than not, I have no idea where I am going on this path I call Life. I believe with every fiber of my Essence that God, "Creator of All That Is," is guiding me to fulfill my life's purpose here on Planet Earth. All I need to do is to continue to trust the signs and that inner Divine Voice that I call *intuition*. I will continue to do my best to be kind and "Shine my Light" on all living beings, *knowing* I will arrive home safely.

"Oh, and God…I don't remember how many times you whispered in my ear and told me to keep writing this book. Well I'm here to tell you, I have now completed it. Hurray! What's next?"

About The Author

Diane E. Zander, also known as *Heart Moon*, draws from a variety of educational and background experiences as a Registered Nurse, Behavioral Health Consultant, Reiki Master, Inspirational Teacher and Intuitive Photographer. She graduated from the University of Vermont receiving a BS degree in Biology and the William Paterson University receiving a BSN degree in Nursing.

Diane has been spiritually guided in her recent international travels to explore specific locations around the world. In trusting her intuition, even when confronted with death on various occasions, she has gained powerful life lessons and transformational insights.

During these remarkable adventures, Ms. Zander has been gifted to experience and photograph mystifying and unexplainable light phenomena, that she describes as "Photographic Energy Phenomena" or PEP for short.

Diane being a true humanitarian and healer has a strong desire to help others through her life's work. She offers inspirational workshops and facilitates conferences and events to convey greater understanding to people about how our universe works towards restoring our lives.

With the publishing of *Intuitive Adventures beyond the Camera Lens,* Ms. Zander now adds the role of "author" to her resume.

Diane is the founder and president of Heart Moon Institute and Heart Moon Photography and currently resides on the Big Island of Hawaii enjoying precious moments with her friends including the loving majestic beings of the sea, the dolphins and whales.

For further information regarding PEP, please visit:

www.heartmoonphotography.com